FRANKENSTEIN

by Mary Shelley

Literature Guide Developed by Angela F. Antrim
for *Secondary Solutions*®

ISBN-10: 0-9845205-2-X
ISBN-13: 978-0-9845205-2-7

Secondary ◆ *Solutions*
THE *FIRST* SOLUTION FOR THE SECONDARY TEACHER®
WWW.4SECONDARYSOLUTIONS.COM

Frankenstein Literature Guide

About This Literature Guide

Secondary Solutions is the endeavor of a high school English teacher who could not seem to find appropriate materials to help her students master the necessary concepts at the secondary level. She grew tired of spending countless hours researching, creating, writing, and revising lesson plans, worksheets, quizzes, tests, and extension activities to motivate and inspire her students, and at the same time, address those ominous content standards. Materials that were available were either juvenile in nature, skimpy in content, or were moderately engaging activities that did not come close to meeting the content standards on which her students were being tested. Frustrated and tired of trying to get by with inappropriate, inane lessons, she finally decided that if the right materials were going to be available to her and other teachers, she was going to have to make them herself. Mrs. Bowers set to work to create one of the most comprehensive and innovative Literature Guide sets on the market. Joined by a middle school teacher with 21 years of secondary school experience, Secondary Solutions began, and has matured into a specialized team of intermediate and secondary teachers who have developed for you a set of materials unsurpassed by all others.

Before the innovation of Secondary Solutions, materials that could be purchased offered a reproducible student workbook and a separate set of teacher materials at an additional cost. Other units provided the teacher with student materials only, and very often, the content standards were ignored. Secondary Solutions provides all of the necessary materials for complete coverage of the literature units of study, including author biographies, pre-reading activities, numerous and varied vocabulary and comprehension activities, study-guide questions, graphic organizers, literary analysis and critical thinking activities, essay and writing ideas, extension activities, quizzes, unit tests, alternative assessment, and much more. Each Guide is designed to address the unique learning styles and comprehension levels of every student in your classroom. All materials are written and presented at the grade level of the learner, and include *extensive coverage of the content standards*. As an added bonus, all teacher materials are included.

As a busy teacher, you don't have time to waste reinventing the wheel. You want to get down to the business of *teaching*. With our professionally developed teacher-written Literature Guides, Secondary Solutions has provided you with the answer to your time management problems, while saving you hours of tedious and exhausting work. Our Guides will allow you to focus on the most important aspects of teaching—the personal, one-on-one, hands-on instruction you enjoy most—the reason you became a teacher in the first place.

Secondary **Solutions**
The *First* Solution for the Secondary Teacher®
www.4secondarysolutions.com

How to Use Our Literature Guides

Our Literature Guides are based upon the *National Council of the Teachers of English* and the *International Reading Association's* national English/Language Arts Curriculum and Content Area Standards. The materials we offer allow you to teach the love and full enjoyment of literature, while still addressing the concepts upon which your students are assessed.

These Guides are designed to be used in their sequential entirety, or may be divided into separate parts. **Please do not feel pressure to use everything as is!** We have worked hard to create a variety of helpful materials for you to choose from. Pick and choose materials that fit the needs of *your* students in *your* classroom, in *your* timeframe! The important thing is that the work has been done for you, and you are not forced into extra work.

There are several distinct categories within each Literature Guide:
- *Exploring Expository Writing*—Worksheets designed to address the exploration and analysis of functional and/or informational materials and of the historical aspects of the text
    - ✓ *Author Biography,* including heritage, beliefs, and customs of the author
    - ✓ *Historical Context,* including allusions and unique diction, comparison of situations across historical eras, analysis of theme relevant to the historical era
    - ✓ *Biographies of relevant non-fictional characters*
- **Comprehension Check**—Similar to *Exploring Expository Writing,* but designed for comprehension of narrative text—study questions designed to guide students *as they read the text.*
    - ✓ Questions focus on *Reading Comprehension and Analysis* and cover a wide range of questioning based on Bloom's Taxonomy
- *Standards Focus*—Worksheets and activities that directly address the content standards and allow students extensive practice in literary skills and analysis. *Standards Focus* activities are found within every chapter or section. Some examples:
    - ✓ *Literary Response and Analysis,* including *Figurative Language, Irony, Flashback, Theme, Tone and Mood, Style,* and *Aesthetic Approach,* etc.
    - ✓ *Writing Strategies,* including developing thesis statements, audience and purpose, sentence combining, concise word choice, developing research questions, etc.
- **Assessment Preparation**—Vocabulary activities which emulate the types of vocabulary/ grammar proficiency on which students are tested in state and national assessments. *Assessment Preparation* activities are found within every chapter or section. Some examples:
    - ✓ *Writing Conventions,* including *Parts of Speech, Precise Word Choice, Punctuation*
    - ✓ *Vocabulary and Word Development,* including *Context Clues, Connotation/Denotation, Word Roots, Analogies, Literal and Figurative Language*
- *Quizzes and Tests*—Quizzes are included for each chapter or designated section; final tests as well as alternative assessment are available at the end of each Guide.
- *Pre-Reading, Post-Reading Activities, Essay/Writing Ideas plus Sample Rubrics*—Each Guide also has its own unique pre-reading, post reading, and essay/writing ideas and alternative assessment activities.

Each Guide contains handouts and activities for varied levels of difficulty. We know that not all students are alike—nor are all teachers! We hope you can effectively utilize every aspect our Literature Guides have to offer—we want to make things easier on you. If you need additional assistance, please email us at info@4secondarysolutions.com. Thank you for choosing Secondary Solutions—The *First* Solution for the Secondary Teacher®.

Frankenstein
Pre-Reading Ideas and Activities

*The following are suggested activities to supplement the study of **Frankenstein** before reading the novel.*

1. Research/define each of the following terms which relate in some way to the novel: autodidact (the creature is said to be a clever autodidact), Cornelis Agrippa, the story of Columbus and his egg, galvanism, philospher's stone, golem, Lord Byron, Erasmus Darwin, hubris, myth of Narcissus, myth of Pygmalion, myth of Prometheus, alchemy, spontaneous generation, physiognomy.
2. Read Mary Wollstonecraft's *A Vindication of the Rights of Woman* (1796). Write an essay summarizing Wollstonecraft's views.
3. Read William Godwin's *Enquiry Concerning Political Justice* (1812). Write an essay summarizing Godwin's views.
4. Research the scientific history of creating life via cloning and in vitro fertilization. Share what you learn in an oral presentation to the class.
5. Learn about the importance of human companionship from a psychological point of view. Examine how people react when they are shunned by society. Share what you learn in an oral presentation to the class.
6. Research a group of people (lepers, India's untouchables, AIDS victims, etc.) who have been historically shunned by society. Learn how others may now be working to assist these people. Create a poster or other visual presentation to share what you learn.
7. Write a brief narrative in which a main character struggles with his/her feelings of loneliness. Perform the dramatic narrative for the class.
8. Read Percy Bysshe Shelley's *The Necessity of Atheism* (1812) or *Prometheus Unbound: A Lyrical Drama* (1820). Write an essay summarizing the work.
9. Research Hans Christian Orsted's work regarding the connection between electricity and magnetism. Write a report to share what you learn.
10. Read another novel by Mary Shelley: *Valperga* (1823), *The Last Man* (1826), *The Fortunes of Perkin Warbeck* (1830), *Falkner* (1837). Write an essay summarizing the novel.
11. Read poetry by the Romantic poets Percy Bysshe Shelley, Lord Byron, William Wordsworth, Samuel Taylor Coleridge, and John Keats. Select a poem by each poet to orally perform for the class.
12. Read a Gothic novel: *Vathek* by Beckford (1787), *Mysteries of Udolpho* by Radcliffe (1794), *Tales of Terror* by Lewis (1799), *The Castle of Otranto* by Walpole (1754), *Dracula* by Stoker (1897). Write an essay summarizing the novel.
13. Read a science fiction novel: *Gulliver's Travels* by Swift (1796), *Journey to the Center of the Earth* by Verne (1870), *The Invisible Man* by Wells (1897), *Foundation* by Asimov (1951), *The War of the Worlds* by Wells (1898), *Contact* by Sagan (1985).
14. Create a detailed map of Switzerland including the country's main cities, lakes, and mountains.
15. Learn about the geological forces that created the mountains and glaciers of Switzerland. Create a poster to visually share what you learn.

Pre-Reading Activity: Biological Scientific Research

Directions: *For the following statements and questions, compose several sentences or a paragraph giving your reaction or answer to each question on a separate piece of paper. Do you agree? Disagree? Why or why not?*

Scientists continually explore and learn about the process of creating human life.

1. In in vitro fertilization, an egg is fertilized outside the womb and then implanted into a uterus. This breakthrough in fertilization resulted in approximately 7,423 live births in the United States in 2007.

    a. Describe the benefits or positive results of in vitro fertilization.

    b. Discuss several ethical or moral concerns people may raise regarding in vitro fertilization.

2. Cloning, the process of creating duplicate biological material, began in 1997 when Scottish scientists cloned Dolly the sheep.

    a. List ways that cloning could be utilized to benefit humanity.

    b. Identify several ethical or moral concerns people may raise regarding cloning.

3. Stem cells are capable of developing into a wide variety of specialized cells in the body. According to research, stem cells could replace damaged cells in human beings, potentially curing disease or allowing for the creation of organs.

    a. Name ways that stem cell research and its results could benefit humanity.

    b. Give examples of any ethical or moral concerns people may raise regarding stem cell research.

4. Scientists studying the human genome are working to map the location of each gene and chromosome which can be genetically passed from parent to child. Scientifically, this could mean that parents could decide the eye color of their unborn child, or their academic or athletic ability.

    a. Generalize ways that human genome mapping could benefit humanity.

    b. Summarize the ethical or moral issues people may raise regarding human genome mapping.

5. Select one topic (in vitro fertilization, cloning, stem cell research, mapping the human genome) to investigate further. Share what you learned in a research report or paper.

Frankenstein
Journal Topics

Prologue: Discuss your reaction to the conditions under which Mary Shelley wrote *Frankenstein*. Does Mary Shelley's age when she wrote the book surprise you? Are you surprised at the other participants in the contest? Why or why not?

Letters: Explain several of the characteristics of literary Romanticism and provide examples of how these characteristics appear in modern-day literature.

Chapter 1: Evaluate Victor's feelings for and reaction to Elizabeth Lavenza. Do you think that they have a normal, healthy relationship? Why or why not?

Chapter 2: Predict how Victor's solitary tendencies and academic interests will come to fruition in his later behavior.

Chapter 3: How does Victor's relationship with his mother influence the way he views and treats Elizabeth? Do you think Victor would have enjoyed a relationship with a more independent woman? Why or why not?

Chapter 4: The Romantic writers valued nature over technology. Discuss how modern-day society would be different if 20th-century people had chosen to have the same values.

Chapter 5: Why do you think that Victor reacts as he does when the creature comes to life? Are you surprised or disappointed by Victor's reaction? How do you think you would have reacted in the same situation?

Chapter 6: Discuss the similarities between the lives and personalities of Justine Moritz, Elizabeth Lavenza, and Caroline Frankenstein.

Chapter 7: If Victor had been with William, do you think that the creature would still have killed William? Would the creature have killed Victor instead? Why or why not?

Chapter 8: Victor does not share the information that he suspects about William's murderer. What does this choice say about Victor's personality and values?

Chapter 9: In your opinion, how did Victor's initial reaction to the creature influence the creature's actions? If Victor had acted more kindly to the creature, would the creature have been able to integrate into society?

Chapter 10: The creature uses threats to try to control Victor. Do you think that the creature could have more effectively interacted with Victor? How?

Chapter 11: By describing his first experiences, does the creature alter the reader's opinion of him? Why or why not?

Chapter 12: Compare and contrast the Frankenstein and DeLacey families.

Chapter 13: Evaluate how human the creature is. Decide if the creature should or should not be classified as a human. Explain the reasons for your answer.

Chapter 14: Which is the strongest female character in the novel: Caroline, Elizabeth, Agatha, Safie? Which is the weakest female character? Explain the reasons for your answers.

Chapter 15: The creature responds emotionally to the books he finds in Victor's coat. If *Frankenstein* were written in the 21st century, what books would most likely garner a strong reaction in the creature? Explain why you selected each book.

Chapter 16: Is it fair and/or appropriate for the creature to blame his actions on humans' reception of him? Why or why not?

Chapter 17: Predict what will occur if Victor makes a mate for the creature.

Chapter 18: Evaluate Victor as person. How likable is he? Would you want him for a friend? Explain your answers.

Chapter 19: Mary Shelley selects landscapes to mirror the characters' feelings and actions. What location would have been appropriate if Victor had excitedly gone about creating a female creature? Explain your answer.

Chapter 20: The creature attempts to control Victor through fear and threats. Do you think the creature could have attained his desired results by attempting a different approach? What approach do you think would have worked? Explain your answers.

Chapter 21: Victor is shocked by Clerval's death. Does Victor's reaction seem appropriate or do you think Victor should have anticipated the creature killing his friend? Explain your answer.

Chapter 22: Victor tells his father, "A thousand times would I have shed my own blood, drop by drop, to have saved their lives. . ." (184) Do you think that Victor would have truly sacrificed his life for his friends and family? Why or why not?

Chapter 23: Evaluate Victor's reaction to the creature's actions. Does Victor rightly place blame where it is due? How culpable should Victor feel regarding the creature's actions?

Chapter 24: Victor's scientific knowledge led to several murders. What factors might have influenced how Victor's knowledge was used? Could Victor's experiments been used for good? Why or why not?

Continuation: How do you think the creature would have acted if he had experienced companionship?

Standards Focus: Author Biography
Mary Shelley

Mary Wollstonecraft Godwin Shelley was born in London, England on August 30, 1797, into a well-known literary family. Shelley's mother, Mary Wollstonecraft, died shortly after giving birth to her. Mary Wollstonecraft had already received recognition as the early feminist writer of *A Vindication of the Rights of Women*. This left young Mary Godwin to be raised by her father, William Godwin, the author of *Enquiry Concerning Political Justice*. Because of his beliefs, Godwin and his family were often surrounded by progressive radicals, writers, and poets such as Thomas Paine, William Blake, Samuel Taylor Coleridge, and Percy Shelley, who had been expelled from Oxford for refusing to admit that he penned *The Necessity of Atheism*.

As a teenager, Mary Shelley read voraciously and soaked in the conversations of the intellectuals that her father entertained. One of these men, poet Percy Bysshe Shelley, took an interest in the teenaged Mary. In 1814, at the age of sixteen, Mary Godwin ran away with twenty-two-year-old Percy Bysshe Shelley, who happened to be married at the time. This action strained Mary's relationship with her father, and the two did not speak for several years. While Mary and Percy toured Europe during their tempestuous and impulsive relationship, Percy continued sporadically seeing his wife, Harriet. Percy's marriage ended in November 1816 when Harriet, pregnant with her husband's child, drowned herself in London. The next month, on December 30, 1816, Mary Godwin and Percy Shelley married.

Throughout their relationship, Percy and his literary friends influenced Mary and her writing. While visiting the British writer Lord Byron in Switzerland in the summer of 1816, Mary, Percy, and Lord Byron decided to pass the time by engaging in a contest to determine who could write the best ghost story. Eighteen-year-old Mary's story of a scientist who constructs a repulsive monster evolved into the novel *Frankenstein* and won Mary the prize over the two older and more seasoned authors. After Mary completed the novel, Percy Shelley edited *Frankenstein* and wrote its preface in Mary's voice. When the book was published anonymously in three volumes in 1818, it became an instant bestseller. Later, in 1823, *Frankenstein* was reprinted in two volumes bearing Mary Shelley's name as the author.

From 1815-1819, Mary and Percy Shelley had four children, only one of whom survived childhood. In 1822, Mary became a single parent to young William Shelley when Percy Shelley drowned in a boating accident off the coast of Italy. Mary continued to write, publishing *Valperga* in 1823, *The Last Man* in 1826, *The Fortunes of Perkin Warbeck* in 1830, and *Falkner* in 1837. She also edited the works of her husband after his death. After residing with her son and his wife for several years, Mary Wollstonecraft Godwin Shelley died in London in 1851. She was buried alongside her parents in the churchyard of St. Peters in Bournemouth, England.

Name _____ Period _____

Comprehension Check: Exploring Expository Writing—Author Biography

Directions: *Using the article about Mary Shelley on page 10, complete the following worksheet. Be sure to answer each question using complete sentences.*

1. Explain how Mary's upbringing influenced young Mary and her life. _____

   _____

   _____

   _____

2. Evaluate Mary and Percy's initial relationship in terms of nineteenth century morality. How do you think Mary and Percy would have been received by traditional society? How do Mary and Percy's radical backgrounds set the stage for their relationship to occur? _____

   _____

   _____

   _____

   _____

   _____

   _____

3. Tell how Percy Shelley impacted and influenced Mary Shelley's writing. _____

   _____

   _____

4. Infer why *Frankenstein* was originally published anonymously. _____

   _____

   _____

5. List three books that Mary Shelley wrote and the year in which they were published.

   _____

   _____

   _____

   _____

   _____

Standards Focus: Genre—Romanticism and the Gothic/Science Fiction Novel

Mary Shelley's *Frankenstein* (1818) draws heavily on the British Romantic and Gothic traditions, while her use of science and technology positions the young author's creation as one of the first science fiction novels.

Literary **Romanticism** began in earnest with William Wordsworth and Samuel Taylor Coleridge's *Lyrical Ballads* (1798) and Johann Wolfgang von Goethe's *Faust* (1808). Springing from the ideals of the French and American Revolutions, Romanticism embraced the progressive movement that paralleled the scientific and Industrial Revolutions. Romantic writers frequently wrote about nature, travel, folklore, and legends—aspects which Shelley incorporates into *Frankenstein*. On a personal level, the Romantics traditionally stood against authoritarian governments and rejected conservative morality. Writers emphasized individualism, feelings of personal expression, and emotional responses to life experience. Mary Shelley's personal interactions with the Romantic writers Percy Bysshe Shelley, Lord Byron, and William Blake strongly influenced *Frankenstein* and the young author even incorporated excerpts from Coleridge's *The Rime of the Ancient Mariner* (1798) into *Frankenstein*.

A prolific reader as a teenager, Mary Godwin Shelley read many **Gothic** novels including Beckford's *Vathek* (1787), Radcliffe's *Mysteries of Udolpho* (1794), and Lewis's *Tales of Terror* (1799). The literary Gothic tradition began in 1754 with Horace Walpole's *The Castle of Otranto*. Known for incorporating mysterious elements into the text, Gothic novels frequently occur in creepy, far-away settings and feature supernatural characters, haunted houses, castles, darkness, death, curses, and secrets. Victor Frankenstein's dark and secretive act of searching for body parts to use in his scientific research, as well as the novel's locales of Switzerland, the Orkney Islands, and the Arctic, place *Frankenstein* firmly in the Gothic vein which continues through Bram Stoker's *Dracula* (1897) and into many modern-day novels.

While Johannes Kepler's *Somnium* (1634), a fantasy of lunar astronomy, and Jonathan Swift's *Gulliver's Travels* (1726) began the genre of **science fiction**, Mary Shelley's *Frankenstein* and *The Last Man* (1826) coalesced to create the form of the modern-day science fiction novel. Marked by their use of scientific principles and modern technology, science fiction evolved through Jules Verne's legacy, beginning with *A Journey to the Centre of the Earth* (1864), H.G. Wells's *The War of the Worlds* (1898), to the "Golden Age of Science Fiction" (1930s-1950s) which includes Isaac Asimov's *Foundation* series (1942-1950) and John W. Campbell's popular science fiction magazine *Astounding Science Fiction*. Modern science fiction writers include Asimov (*I, Robot*, 1951), Arthur C. Clarke (*2001: A Space Odyssey*, 1967, and *Venus Prime* Series), Kurt Vonnegut (*Slaughterhouse Five*, 1969; *Cat's Cradle*, 1963), and Michel Crichton (*The Andromeda Strain*, 1969; *Jurassic Park*, 1990)

Mary Shelley's use of distant settings coupled with technological innovation places *Frankenstein* in the Romantic tradition of the Gothic novel and begins modern-day science fiction.

Name _____ Period _____

Comprehension Check: Exploring Expository Writing—Genre

Directions: *After reading the article about genres on page 12, answer the following questions in complete sentences.*

1. What topics did the Romantic writers frequently incorporate into their work? _____

    _____

    _____

2. How did Mary and Percy Bysshe Shelley's personal relationship demonstrate their

    adherence to the personal values embraced by the Romantics? Refer to the

    biography of Mary Shelley for information regarding her personal relationship with

    Percy Shelley. _____

    _____

    _____

    _____

3. How does Mary Shelley incorporate aspects of the Gothic novel into *Frankenstein*?

    _____

    _____

    _____

    _____

4. Name a modern-day Gothic novel and explain how it continues in the Gothic tradition.

    _____

    _____

    _____

5. List two characteristics of science fiction novels. _____

    _____

    _____

6. Select your favorite science fiction novel or movie. Explains how it incorporates the

    aspects of science fiction. _____

    _____

    _____

    _____

    _____

Standards Focus: Mythology
Frankenstein, or the Modern Prometheus

When titling her novel *Frankenstein, or the Modern Prometheus*, Mary Shelley firmly placed her writing in the tradition of the mythological Prometheus.

According to ancient Greek mythology, Prometheus sprang from the Titans Iapetus and Themis. After the Titans fell to the Olympians, Zeus, the Olympian leader, pardoned Prometheus and allowed him to continue living among the gods. When Prometheus created the first humans from clay, an angry Zeus denied fire to the earth's newest inhabitants. In an act of defiance, Prometheus stole fire from the gods and gave it to humans so they could warm themselves and cook food. Thus, Prometheus takes on the role of a creator, much as Victor Frankenstein creates his immortal monster.

Due to their interest in folklore and legends, the Romantic writers frequently incorporated Promethean allusions into their works. In 1815, a young Mary Shelley read Ovid's *Metamorphosis*, verse that refers to Prometheus forming humans from clay. William Blake visually referred to Prometheus in the illustrations for "Visions of the Daughters of Albion," while Johann Wolfgang Goethe wrote a verse drama entitled *Prometheus* (1789). Even more influential to Mary Shelley, both Lord Byron and Percy Bysshe Shelley, with whom Mary spent the summer of 1816, created literary works based on the Promethean myth. That summer, Byron wrote a poem entitled "Prometheus" and also referred to the Titan in his novel, *Manfred* (1817). In 1816, Percy Shelley reread Aeschylus's play *Prometheus Bound* and wrote a rebuttal, *Prometheus Unbound*, a four-act play, which was published in 1820.

Mary Shelley's allusions to Prometheus, as well as aspects of her relationship with Percy Shelley, come to life in *Frankenstein*. The novel's protagonist Victor Frankenstein was named after Percy Shelley's penname of choice, Victor, which the writer used for his first publication, *Original Poetry by Victor and Cazire* (1810). In *Frankenstein*, Victor Frankenstein portrays the role of a Promethean creator when he forms a living being out of inanimate parts. Frankenstein also utilizes lightning, a form of fire, to bring his creature to life. In 19th century society, Shelley's idea of Victor Frankenstein as a giver of life was considered blasphemous since it presented a human taking God's place as the creator of living things.

By drawing on Promethean mythology, Mary Shelley portrays Victor Frankenstein as a maverick artist who has the ability to create life.

Name _____ Period _____

Comprehension Check: Exploring Expository Writing—Mythology

Directions: *After reading the article about Mythology on page 14, answer the following questions in complete sentences.*

1. Summarize the Greek myth of Prometheus. _____

   _____

   _____

   _____

2. Explain how Lord Byron and Percy Bysshe Shelley influenced Mary Shelley's choice to

   write a Promethean-inspired story. _____

   _____

   _____

   _____

   _____

3. Besides Byron and Shelley, name two other Romantic writers who alluded to

   Prometheus in their writing. _____

   _____

   _____

4. How does Mary Shelley embody Percy Shelley in *Frankenstein*? _____

   _____

   _____

   _____

5. Name two ways that Victor Frankenstein acts as Prometheus in *Frankenstein*.

   _____

   _____

   _____

6. Name a modern-day book or movie and explain how it alludes to Greek mythology.

   _____

   _____

   _____

   _____

Standards Focus: Allusions, Terminology, and Expressions

Prologue

- *Iliad* (9)- a Greek epic poem by Homer describing the siege of Troy
- *The Tempest* (9)- a comedy by English playwright William Shakespeare in which a duke is banished to an island
- *A Midsummer Night's Dream* (9)- a comedy by English playwright William Shakespeare in which a group of lovers are enchanted by fairies when they spend the night in a forest
- *Paradise Lost* (9)- Epic poem by John Milton about the Fall of Man
- **Geneva** (10)- a city that sits by the Lake of Geneva in Switzerland

Letters

- **sledges** (13)- sleighs that travel over snow
- **stage-coach** (13)- horse-drawn coach that carries passengers and/or parcels
- **St. Petersburgh** (13)- Russian seaport in the Gulf of Finland off the Baltic Sea
- **Archangel** (13)- Russian seaport on Dvina Bay
- **fortnight** (13)- two weeks
- **gales** (17)- very strong winds
- **sea-room** (18)- unobstructed space at sea in which a vessel can be easily maneuvered

Chapter One

- **Lucerne** (27)- a Swiss city on the Lake of Lucerne
- **Reuss** (28)- a river that runs through the city of Lucerne
- **plaited** (28)- braided straw or animal hair, usually for baskets or rugs
- **vale** (30)- a valley

Chapter Two

- **filial** (34)- pertaining to a son or daughter's relationship with his/her parents
- **shrine-dedicated** (35)- intended or used as a sacred place
- **Cornelius Agrippa** (36)- German magician, theologian, astronomer, occult

writer, and alchemist; often persecuted for being a heretic for his belief in the occult
- **Paracelsus** (36)- Renaissance physician, occultist, botanist, alchemist, and astrologer; devoted to the construction of astrological charms to cure disease
- **philosopher's stone** (37)- a substance sought by alchemists that would be capable of changing metals into gold or silver and of prolonging life
- **elixir of life** (37)- alchemic preparation believed to be capable of prolonging life
- **slough** (37)- condition of despair or hopelessness; a spiritual low point
- **galvanism** (38)- the application of electricity to the body

Chapter Three

- **Ingolstadt** (40)- city in the Bavarian region of southern Germany
- **scarlet fever** (40)- disease caused by strep and characterized by high fever and red cheeks
- **Angel of Destruction** (43)- Satan
- **alchemists** (43)- people who studied a form of chemistry and speculative philosophy practiced in the Middle Ages and the Renaissance which was concerned with finding the elixir of life and changing metal into gold or silver
- **natural science** (44)- a science or knowledge of objects or processes observable in nature, such as biology or physics

Chapter Four

- **precepts** (51)- commands and directions
- **alloy** (54)- anything that serves to reduce quality or purity; a mixture of metals

Chapter Five

- **Dante** (56)- Italian author of *The Inferno (c.1300)*, a book that discusses punishments for specific crimes of morality

- *The Vicar of Wakefield* (58)- a 1766 novel by Irish author Oliver Goldsmith
- **florins** (58)- gold coins
- **"without Greek"** (58)- without an education; without use or knowledge of academics
- **spectre** (59)- visible ghost, phantom, or apparition
- **bosom** (60)- the chest of a human being

Chapter Six

- **fetter** (62)- anything that confines or restrains
- **republican** (63)- pertaining to a government in which the supreme power rests in the body of citizens entitled to vote and is exercised by representatives chosen directly or indirectly by them
- **Ariosto** (63)- Italian poet who lived from 1474–1533 and wrote *Orlando Furioso*
- **Angelica** (63) - In *Orlando Furioso* (1532), Orlando's obsession with Angelica drives him mad
- **phraseology** (64)- manner or style of speaking
- **Adieu** (65)- Goodbye, Farewell
- **oriental** (67)- Asian
- **dialects** (67)- variations of a spoken language

Chapter Seven

- **Lausanne** (73)- Swiss city on the northern shore of Lake Geneva
- **Jura** (73)- mountain range between France and Switzerland
- **Mont Blanc** (73)- mountain peak in France—the highest peak in the Alps
- **league** (74)- unit of distance covering approximately three miles
- **Salêve** (74)- a mountain that towers over Geneva, Switzerland
- **Alps of Savoy** (74)- range of the western Alps in southeast France
- **Belrive** (74)- area on the west banks of Lake Geneva about four miles from the city of Geneva
- **Copêt** (74)- Swiss village near Lake Geneva
- **rustic** (76)- simple, unsophisticated

- **magistrate** (78)- a minor judicial officer having jurisdiction to try minor criminal cases and to conduct preliminary examinations of persons charged with serious crimes
- **deposition** (78)- legal testimony given under oath
- **vulgar** (78)- common
- **acquittal** (79)- being discharged or found not guilty of a crime
- **asylum** (82)- refuge; retreat
- **bauble** (83)- cheap ornament or trinket
- **excommunication** (85)- cut off from communion and sacraments of the church
- **perish on the scaffold** (86)- to be hung until dead
- **morrow** (86)- the next day; tomorrow
- **thrice-accursed** (87)- cursed or doomed three times

Chapter Nine

- **Andes** (90)- mountain range that extends along the western coast of South America
- **Arve** (92)- river that flows through France and Switzerland
- **Omnipotence** (92)- God; a higher power

Chapter Ten

- **anon** (94)- at once; immediately
- **Montanvert** (95)- one of the three large glaciers on Mont Blanc
- **"We rest; a dream has power . . . Nought may endure but mutability!"** (96)- the last stanza of Percy Shelley's poem "Mutability"; stating *nothing stays the same except change*
- **maw** (97)- symbolic center of a voracious hunger or appetite

Chapter Eleven

- **slaked** (101)- satisfied a thirst
- **thrush** (102)- medium-sized brown songbird
- **offals** (103)- inedible parts of a butchered animal
- **quitting** (104)- departing from; leaving
- **Pandaemonium** (104)- the capital of Hell in Milton's *Paradise Lost*

- **kennel** (105)- a wretched abode; a dilapidated house
- **aught** (107)- any part of
- **tapers** (108)- slender candles

Chapter Twelve

- **gait** (111)- manner of walking, stepping, or running
- **out-house** (112)- outbuilding separate from the main structure, usually for a toilet
- **ass** (114)- donkey

Chapter Thirteen

- **faculty** (116)- inherent capability of the body
- **herbage** (117)- leaves and stems of plants
- **Volney's** *Ruins of Empires* (118)- text that elaborated the revolutionary thoughts of Volney, a Napoleonic senator
- **lichen** (119)- greenish fungus/algae that grows on rocks and trees
- **intercourse** (119)- dealings with other people; conversations
- **sallies** (119)- activities or flights of fancy (imagination)

Chapter Fourteen

- **Mahomet** (123)- Mohammed; Arab prophet who founded Islam
- **Lyons** (123)- city in eastern France
- **Mont Cenis** (123)- mountain pass in the Alps between southeastern France and Italy
- **Leghorn** (123)- seaport in western Italy; Livorno
- **meed** (125)- reward; recompense

Chapter Fifteen

- **leathern portmanteau** (127)- leather trunk or suitcase
- *Plutarch's Lives* (127)- a collection of short biographies of the leading political figures of ancient Greece and Rome, by Plutarch (c. 46-120)
- *The Sorrows of Werter* (127)- novel by Goethe in which a young man commits suicide because of unrequited love

- **Numa** (129)- second king of Rome who lived from 715-673 BCE
- **Solon** (129)- poet and statesman in ancient Athens
- **Lycurgus** (129)- statesman in ancient Athens
- **Romulus** (129)- legendary founder of Rome with his brother, Remus
- **Theseus** (129)- ancient Athenian hero who slays the minotaur

Chapter Sixteen

- **stag-like** (135)- resembling an adult male deer
- **arch-fiend** (135)- a main cruel or wicked person; antagonist
- **heath** (138)- tract of land covered with low shrubbery
- **bedewed** (139)- covered, as if with dew
- **Syndic** (141)- a civil magistrate having different powers in different countries

Chapter Seventeen

- **ice-rifts** (144)- open space or fissure between glaciers or large pieces of ice
- **fare** (145)- food; diet
- **compassionated** (146)- showed pity for
- **nought** (148)- nothing

Chapter Eighteen

- **solemnisation** (150)- performance of a marriage ceremony
- **bourne** (153)- destination; goal
- **Rhine** (154)- a river flowing from Switzerland through Germany and the Netherlands into the North Sea
- **Rotterdam** (154)- a seaport in the Netherlands
- **Manheim** (154)- a city in southwestern Germany at the confluence of the Rhine and Neckar rivers; Mannheim
- **Strasburgh** (154)- a city in northeastern France on the Rhine; Strasbourg
- **Mayence** (154)- French city; Mainz
- **Fairyland** (154)- mythical land in Edmund Spenser's *The Faerie Queene (1590-1596)*
- **Uri** (154)- lake in central Switzerland
- **waterspout** (155)- tornado that occurs over open water

- **La Valais** (155)- mountainous canton in Switzerland
- **Pays de Vaud** (155)- Swiss canton in which Lausanne is located
- **cataract** (155)- a series of small waterfalls with one vertical drop
- **Cologne** (156)- city in western Germany
- **Holland** (156)- country that borders the North Sea; Netherlands
- **white cliffs** (156)- white cliffs of Dover on the southeastern coast of England
- **Thames** (156)- river that flows through London to the North Sea
- **Tilbury Fort** (156)- fort that lies on the River Thames designed to protect England from a sea invasion
- **Gravesend** (156)- seaport in southeastern England on the Thames River
- **Woolwich** (156)- a former borough of Greater London, England, now part of Greenwich and Newham; royal military academy and arsenal
- **Greenwich** (156)- a borough in southeastern London, England; located on the prime meridian from which geographic longitude is measured
- **St. Paul's** (156)- cathedral in London
- **Tower** (156)- Tower of London; a historic fortress in London, England: originally a royal palace, later a prison, now an arsenal and museum

Chapter Nineteen
- **Perth** (158)- county in central Scotland
- **Edinburgh** (158)- capital of Scotland
- **Windsor** (158)- city in southern England on the Thames River
- **Oxford** (158)- English city located northwest of London
- **Matlock** (158)- city in central England
- **Cumberland lakes** (158)- region of lakes, waters, and mountains in northwestern England
- **Falkland** (159)- 17th century English statesman and poet
- **Goring** (159)- 17th century Royalist commander in the English civil war

- **spires** (159)- a tall, acutely pointed pyramidal roof or roof-like structure on a tower, roof, etc.
- **Hampden** (159)- British statesman who defended the rights of the House of Commons against Charles I
- **Derby** (160)- city in central England
- **Westmoreland** (160) - county in the northwest of England; in 1974, Westmoreland merged with the neighboring county of Cumberland to form Cumbria.
- **Arthur's Seat** (161)- main peak of Holyrood Park in Edinburgh, Scotland
- **St. Bernard's Well** (161)- mineral spring near Stockbridge in Edinburgh, Scotland
- **Pentland Hills** (161)- range of hills to the southwest of Edinburgh, Scotland
- **Coupar** (161)- town in Fifeshire, Scotland
- **St. Andrew's** (161)- city in Fife, Scotland; home to St. Andrews University
- **Tay** (161)- river in the highlands of Scotland

Chapter Twenty
- **sophisms** (164)- arguments intended to deceive someone
- **casement** (165)- a window sash opening on hinges that are generally attached to the upright side of its frame
- **oaten cake** (168)- muffin-like cake made of oats, flour, and water
- **besought** (168)- implored or begged
- **skiff** (169)- boat small enough to be sailed or rowed by one person
- **rudder** (170)- a vertical blade at the stern of a vessel that can be turned horizontally to change the vessel's direction when in motion
- **breakers** (171)- waves

Chapter Twenty–One
- **apothecary** (174)- druggist; pharmacist
- **interment** (174)- the burial of a corpse, usually followed by a ceremony
- **affright** (175)- to frighten
- **gaolers** (176)- jailors; prison guards
- **turnkeys** (176)- persons who have charge of the keys of a prison or jail

- **Orkney Islands** (180)- an island group off the northeastern tip of Scotland
- **Havre-de-Grace** (181)- port city in northwestern France
- **laudanum** (182)- a drug in which opium is the chief ingredient

Chapter Twenty–Two

- **brethren** (183)- fellow members
- **wretch** (183)- person of despicable character
- **"the apple was already eaten, and the angel's arm bared"** (187)- allusion to Milton's *Paradise Lost*; "the apple was already eaten" associates Victor with a fallen Adam who has already eaten the apple in the Garden of Eden"; the angel with the bared arm is Blake, "the Covering Cherub" who is assigned to assure that Victor cannot regress or go back, thus Victor views his creation as an act of divine destiny
- **retard** (187)- to make slow; delay
- **Como** (189)- lake in northern Italy
- **Villa Lavenza** (190)- home belonging to the Lavenza family
- **Evian** (190)- area on the south shore of Lake Geneva in Switzerland
- **Montalègre** (190)- lake in Switzerland
- **Drance** (191)- a tributary of the Rhone River in Switzerland near Evian
- **glens** (191)- small, narrow, secluded valleys
- **amphitheatre** (191)- a level area of oval or circular shape surrounded by rising ground

Chapter Twenty–Three

- **bridal bier** (193)- bed on one's wedding-night; allusion to the 1781 painting *The Nightmare* by Henry Fuseli

- **physiognomy** (197)- the face or countenance, especially when considered as an index to the character
- **auditor** (197)- a hearer; listener
- **martyrs** (198)- persons who undergo severe or constant suffering

Chapter Twenty–Four

- **wont** (199)- accustomed to
- **Mediterranean** (200)- sea surrounded by Africa, Europe, and Asia
- **Black Sea** (200)- a sea between Europe and Asia, bordered by Turkey, Romania, Bulgaria, Ukraine, Georgia, and the Russian Federation
- **Tartary** (200)- region that spans the border of eastern Europe and Asia
- **bedim** (201)- to make dim; darken
- **gibe** (203)- taunting or sarcastic remark
- **Frozen Ocean** (204)- Arctic Ocean
- **ground sea** (204)- a fluid undercurrent of water, which lies below the ice
- **crags** (205)- rough, broken, projecting parts of rocks

Continuation

- **projectors** (208)- people who plan projects or schemes
- **archangel** (208)- chief or principal angel
- **infantine** (209)- infantile; childlike
- **comrades** (210)- companions; associates
- **utility** (212)- usefulness
- **draught** (213)- a drink
- **abortion** (218)- malformed or monstrous person or thing
- **thither** (219)- toward that place or point; there
- **wert** (219)- being; are

Name _____   Period _____

Frankenstein
Vocabulary List

Directions: Use a dictionary to find the meanings of the following words in Frankenstein. Your teacher will direct you to do this lesson either as you read each chapter, or as a pre-reading activity. Whatever method your teacher chooses, be sure to keep this list and your definitions to use in vocabulary exercises and to study for quizzes and tests.

Prologue, Letters
physiological (9)
delineating (9)
expedient (9)
forebodings (10)
satiate (11)
enticement (13)
endowments (15)
solicitude (19)
countenance (21)
melancholy (25)

Chapters One–Two
indefatigable (27)
interment (28)
recompensing (29)
penury (30)
reverential (31)
vehement (34)
ignoble (35)
chimerical (36)
tertiary (37)
ineffectual (39)

Chapters Three–Five
prognosticated (40)
repose (41)
repugnance (42)
reprobated (43)
recapitulation (44)
deference (46)
dogmatism (48)
hinderance (hindrance) (52)
incipient (54)
languor (56)

Chapters Six–Eight
odious (62)
mien (64)
irreparable (72)
placid (73)
dirge (74)
delirium (76)
depravity (78)
candour (candor) (79)
ignominious (80)
approbation (83)

Chapters Nine–Ten
augmenting (88)
base (89)
efface (90)
abyss (91)
epoch (92)
pallid (93)
precipitous (95)
abhorred (96)
diabolically (97)
disdain (98)

Chapters Eleven–Twelve
opaque (101)
emigration (103)
inclemency (105)
purloined (105)
pensive (107)
conjectured (108)
venerable (109)
enigmatic (110)
ardently (111)
arbiters (113)

Chapters Thirteen–Fourteen
verdure (115)
dissipates (116)
cadence (117)
scion (118)
vagabond (119)
tenets (123)
immured (123)
noisome (124)
expostulate (125)
pittance (125)

Chapters Fifteen–Seventeen
deprecate (127)
sagacity (130)
instigate (134)
consternation (134)
wantonly (135)
vestige (137)
succor (138)
epithets (141)
malignity (142)
contemns (144)

Chapters Eighteen–Twenty
enjoined (149)
enfranchised (152)
sedulous (153)
variegated (154)
eminently (155)
blight (157)
precarious (164)
profundity (165)
impotence (166)
inexorable (167)

Chapters Twenty–One–Twenty–Three
supposition (173)
languid (176)
visage (177)
vexations (180)
degradation (183)
imperious (184)
vanquished (186)
enunciation (187)
artifice (190)
reverie (191)

Chapter Twenty–Four, Continuation
abjuration (200)
repast (201)
scoffing (202)
procured (203)
disencumbered (205)
congeal (206)
dispositions (209)
actuated (214)
superfluous (216)
contumely (218)

Name _____   Period _____

Prologue, Letters
Sample Note-Taking and Summarizing: Prologue

To help you keep track of the novel's events as they occur, you will be taking notes using a chart similar to the one below.

Directions: *For each chapter, fill in the chart with the necessary information. An example for the Prologue is completed below. (Note: Except when writing the summary, you do not need to write in complete sentences.)*

Setting	*(A description of where the action occurs.)* The summer of 1816 in Geneva, Switzerland, in a chateau.
Characters	*(List and describe important information about the characters in the chapter.)* Mary Shelley, Percy Bysshe Shelley, and Lord Byron; Claire Clairmont, Lord Byron's mistress, and John Polidori were also present at the chateau that summer.
Summary of the Chapter	*(A 3-5 sentence summary of the chapter.)* Mary Shelley tells of how she came to write Frankenstein as a young girl. She tells of a group of friends engaged in a contest to see who could write the best ghost story. Shelley tells of her struggle to come up with a good story, and of how one night after a late-night talk, she had a "waking dream" in which she was overcome by the terror of her imagination. She put her visions onto paper, and thus began the tale of Frankenstein.
Prediction of Coming Events	*(Make a prediction of what you think will occur in the next chapter.)* The story of Frankenstein will begin, and we will learn what caused such horror in Shelley that fateful night.

Name _____ Period _____

Note-Taking and Summarizing: Letters

Directions: *For each chapter, fill in the chart with the necessary information. (Note: Except when writing the summary, you do not need to write in complete sentences.)*

Setting	
Characters	
Summary of the Letters	Letter 1: Letter 2: Letter 3: Letter 4:
Prediction of Coming Events	

Name _____   Period _____

Prologue, Letters
Comprehension Check

Directions: *To help you understand all aspects of the novel, respond to the following as they relate to the Prologue and Letters. Write your responses on a separate piece of paper using complete sentences.*

Prologue

1. Who wrote the prologue to *Frankenstein*? For what purpose was it written, according to the author?

2. What stories inspired the idea of writing the "ghost stories" that summer?

3. Describe the conversation that triggered the author's "waking dream."

4. Why does the writer say that *Frankenstein* is not "a mere tale of spectres or enchantment"?

5. Which other works about human nature inspired *Frankenstein*'s author?

6. Summarize where and under what conditions Mary Shelley began writing *Frankenstein*.

Letters

1. Show how the Letters frame the upcoming story of Frankenstein.

2. Analyze how Robert Walton's life and travels adhere to the ideals of Romanticism.

3. Explain how Walton educates himself for his sailing adventure.

4. Predict how successful Walton's voyage will be to find an Arctic passage, and the problems he could encounter on his adventure.

5. What does Walton desire when he writes the second letter?

6. Explain why Walton feels particularly fortunate to have secured the master of his ship.

7. Show how the shipmaster's failed love story adheres to the ideals of Romanticism.

8. Infer how Walton's "belief in the marvelous" makes him an ideal listener of Frankenstein's story.

9. Formulate how the setting of the fourth letter is typically Romantic.

10. Tell what the sailors first see in the distance.

11. Describe the man who boards the ship.

12. Explain why the man is in the Arctic.

13. Analyze how the man fulfills Captain Walton's desires.

14. Generalize why the man agrees to tell Walton his story.

15. Evaluate why the man cautions Walton against his "search for knowledge and wisdom."

16. What is Walton's duty as the man tells his story?

Prologue, Letters
Standards Focus: Mood and Tone

Tone refers to the author's attitude toward the subject or audience of a literary work. The author's background, opinions, and personal experiences often contribute to a work's tone. Tone reflects the feelings of the writer, and can affect the emotional response of the reader to the piece. While we have all heard, "Don't use that tone of voice with me!" a writer does not have the advantage of the sound of his voice to reveal the tone of the piece. As we read the words on the page, the author hopes that the words he or she has chosen and the way he or she has arranged those words will help us hear a voice in our heads, supplying the emotional appeal. Tone can be nostalgic, sentimental, moralizing, humorous or serious, personal or impersonal, subjective or objective, casual or passionate, and more.

When learning to recognize tone, it is also important to understand **mood**, a general feeling that is created by the tone. In literature, writers carefully choose their words, wanting the reader to feel love and hate, joy and sadness. etc. **Mood** is *usually* described in expressions of feeling and emotions, such as fear, surprise, anger, hatred, contentment, or jealousy, to name a few.

In short, *tone* is how the author says something, and *mood* is how it affects you, the reader.

Directions: *Complete the chart below, analyzing each excerpt and how it reflects the tone of the text. After examining the passages, answer the questions that follow.*

1. Each of the following excerpts comes from the Prologue of *Frankenstein*. Read each excerpt in the first column carefully, then in the second column, explain how each item demonstrates the author's attitude toward the novel or its audience. An example has been completed for you.

Excerpt	How The Excerpt Reveals the Tone
"The event on which this fiction is founded... not of impossible occurrence."	Shelley tries to give the novel scientific credence and makes the reader feel the story they are about to hear is not so far-fetched or unbelievable.
"It [the story]... affords a point of view to the imagination for the delineating of human passions more comprehensive and commanding than any which the ordinary relations of existing events can yield."	a.
"...the most humble novelist, who seeks to confer or receive amusement from his labours, may, without presumption, apply to prose fiction a license, or rather a rule, from the adoption of which so many exquisite combinations of human feeling have resulted in the highest specimens of poetry."	b.
"The opinions which naturally spring from the character and situation of the hero are by no means to be conceived as existing always in my own conviction..."	c.

"The season was cold and rainy, and in the evenings we crowded around a blazing wood fire, and occasionally amused ourselves with some German stories of ghosts, which happened to fall into our hands. These tales excited in us a playful desire of imitation."	d.

2. Utilizing details from the chart, write a paragraph that describes the general tone of the Prologue.

_____

_____

_____

_____

_____

_____

3. Read the second letter (pp. 14-17) that Robert Walton writes to his sister, Margaret Saville. Use the chart below to gather quotes from the text that convey the **mood** of the passage in regards to Walton's emotional state. Once you have found the excerpt or passage, explain how each item seeks to influence the reader's emotional reaction or feelings toward a character, theme, or the novel as a whole. An example has been completed for you.

Excerpt	How The Excerpt Influences the Mood (How does it make you, the reader, feel?)
"I have no friend, Margaret."	makes the reader feel sympathetic toward Walton

4. Utilizing details from the chart, discuss how the author's description of Robert Walton makes the reader sympathetic to a person's desire for companionship.

_____

_____

_____

_____

5. Read the first two pages of the fourth letter (pp. 18-19) that Robert Walton writes to his sister, Margaret Saville. Use the chart below to gather quotes from the text that convey the **mood** of the passage in regards to the setting of the novel. Once you have found the excerpt or passage, explain how each item seeks to influence the reader's emotional reaction or feelings. An example has been completed for you.

Excerpt	How The Excerpt Influences the Mood
"...we were nearly surrounded by ice, which closed in the ship on all sides, scarcely leaving her the sea-room in which she floated"	shows a sense of danger and foreboding; feeling of suspense

6. Utilizing details from the chart, discuss how the author's description of the setting evokes an eerie mood for the Frankenstein story.

_____

_____

_____

Name _____ Period _____

Prologue, Letters
Assessment Preparation: Vocabulary in Context

Directions: *Each of the following sentences has been taken directly from Mary Shelley's Frankenstein. Read each sentence, then use the context clues to create a definition for the underlined vocabulary word. After writing your own definition of the word, look up the vocabulary word in a dictionary and write down the definition provided. Also, write a sentence that correctly uses the vocabulary word. An example has been completed for you.*

Ex. "The event on which this fiction is founded has been supposed, by Dr. Darwin, and some of the physiological writers of Germany, as not of impossible occurrence." (9)

    a.   Your Definition: <u>related to the power of body or mind</u>

    b.   Dictionary Definition: <u>concerned with the normal functioning of an organism</u>

    c.   Sentence: <u>In biology, we studied the physiological aspects of the human body.</u>

1. "It was recommended by the novelty of the situations which it develops; and, however impossible as a physical fact, affords a point of view to the imagination for the delineating of human passions more comprehensive and commanding than any which the ordinary relations of existing events can yield." (9)

    a.   Your Definition: _____

    b.   Dictionary Definition: _____

    c.   Sentence: _____

            _____

2. "It was commenced partly as a source of amusement, and partly as an expedient for exercising any untried resources of mind." (9)

    a.   Your Definition: _____

    b.   Dictionary Definition: _____

    c.   Sentence: _____

            _____

3. "You will rejoice to hear that no disaster has accompanied the commencement of an enterprise which you have regarded with such evil forebodings." (10)

    a.   Your Definition: _____

    b.   Dictionary Definition: _____

    c.   Sentence: _____

            _____

4. "I shall satiate my ardent curiosity with the sight of a part of the world never before visited, and may tread a land never before imprinted by the foot of man." (11)

    a.   Your Definition: _____

    b.   Dictionary Definition: _____

c. Sentence: _____

_____

5. "My life might have been passed in ease and luxury; but I preferred glory to every <u>enticement</u> that wealth placed in my path." (13)

a. Your Definition: _____

b. Dictionary Definition: _____

c. Sentence: _____

_____

6. "He is an Englishman, and in the midst of national and professional prejudices, unsoftened by cultivation, retains some of the noblest <u>endowments</u> of humanity." (15)

a. Your Definition: _____

b. Dictionary Definition: _____

c. Sentence: _____

_____

7. "Some of my comrades groaned, and my own mind began to grow watchful with anxious thoughts, when a strange sight suddenly attracted our attention, and diverted our <u>solicitude</u> from our own situation." (18-19)

a. Your Definition: _____

b. Dictionary Definition: _____

c. Sentence: _____

_____

8. "His <u>countenance</u> instantly assumed an aspect of the deepest gloom; and he replied, 'To seek one who fled from me.'" (21)

a. Your Definition: _____

b. Dictionary Definition: _____

c. Sentence: _____

_____

9. "Even now, as I commence my task, his full-toned voice swells in my ears; his lustrous eyes dwell on me with all their <u>melancholy</u> sweetness . . ." (25)

a. Your Definition: _____

b. Dictionary Definition: _____

c. Sentence: _____

_____

Name _____   Period _____

Chapters One – Two
Note-Taking and Summarizing

Directions: *For Chapters One and Two, fill in the chart with the necessary information. (Note: Except when writing the summary, you do not need to write in complete sentences.)*

Chapter One	
Setting	
Characters	
Summary of the Chapter	
Prediction of Coming Events	
Chapter Two	
Setting	
Characters	
Summary of the Chapter	
Prediction of Coming Events	

Chapters One – Two
Comprehension Check

Directions: *To help you understand all aspects of the novel, respond to the following as they relate to Chapters One and Two. Write your responses on a separate piece of paper using complete sentences.*

Chapter One

1. Tell how Victor Frankenstein's parents met.

2. Summarize how Mary Shelley interjects her social interest of caring for the poor into *Frankenstein*.

3. Show how Shelley portrays the women, Caroline and Elizabeth, in Chapter One.

4. Describe Victor's childhood.

5. Explain how Elizabeth comes into the Frankenstein home.

6. Assess how Victor feels about Elizabeth.

Chapter Two

1. Tell about Victor's social tendencies and how he interacts with friends.

2. Contrast Victor's academic interests with those of his friend, Henry Clerval.

3. Infer Victor's meaning when he says of his desire to learn about science: "I find it arise, like a mountain river, from ignoble and almost forgotten sources; but, swelling as it proceeded, it became the torrent which, in its course, has swept away all my hopes and joys." (35)

4. Which authors and topics does Victor become obsessed with reading?

5. Generalize how Victor learns about alchemy and natural science. How does this fit with the characteristics of Romanticism?

6. Describe Victor's experience with lightning. How was it a turning point in his life?

7. Explain Victor's destiny. Locate a quote from the novel to support your answer.

Name _____   Period _____

Chapters One – Two
Standards Focus: Character Interactions

A **main character**, or *protagonist*, is the central figure in a literary work. Most of the novel's events revolve around this person. **Subordinate characters** also appear in a literary work, but not to the extent of the protagonist. Subordinate characters frequently interact with or influence the main character. These interactions can shed light on the main character and affect the work's plot.

Directions: *Complete the two graphic organizers about Elizabeth Lavenza and Victor Frankenstein. Then use the details in the organizers to compare and contrast the two characters.*

1. Complete the graphic organizer with specific details regarding Elizabeth Lavenza. Be sure to include how Elizabeth interacts with Victor.

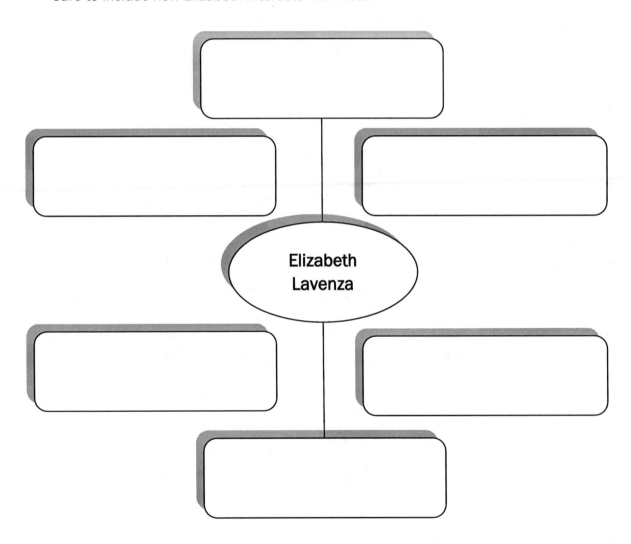

2. Complete the graphic organizer below with specific details regarding Victor Frankenstein.

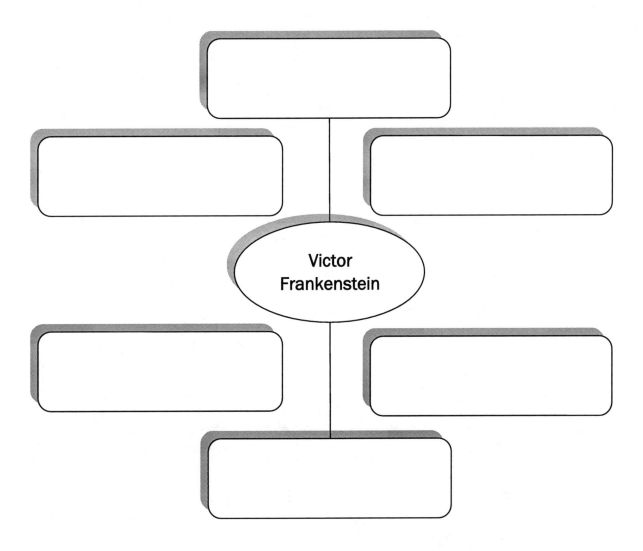

3. Using the information from the graphic organizers, on a separate piece of paper, write several paragraphs comparing and contrasting the personalities of Elizabeth Lavenza and Victor Frankenstein. Be sure to include how Elizabeth and Victor complement each other, as well as how Elizabeth balances Victor's personality.

Chapters One – Two
Assessment Preparation: Spelling, Punctuation, and Capitalization

Directions: *Find the errors in punctuation, capitalization, and spelling for each of the following sentences that contain your vocabulary words from Chapters One and Two. Rewrite the sentences, correcting the errors you find. There is more than one error for each sentence. An example has been done for you. (The vocabulary words used in this exercise appear in bold print.)*

Ex. he was respected by all who new him for his integrity and indefatigable atention to public business?

Corrected: <u>He was respected by all who knew him for his integrity and indefatigable attention to public business.</u>

1. He came like a protecting spirit to the poor girl, who committed herself to his care, and after the **interment** of his freind, he conducted her to geneva, and placed her under the protecion of a relation.

   Corrected: _____

   _____

   _____

   _____

2. There was a show of gratitude and worship in his attachment to my Mother, differing holy from the doating fondness of age, for it was inspired by reverence for her virtues. and a desire to be the means of in some degree **recompensing** her for the sorows she had endured, but which gave inexpressible grace to his behavior to her.

   Corrected: _____

   _____

   _____

   _____

   _____

   _____

3. during one of their walks a poor cot in the folding of a vale attracted there notice as being singularly disconsolate, while the number of half clothed children gathered about it spoke of **penury** in it's worst shape.

   Corrected: _____

   _____

_____

_____

4. The passionate and almost **reverential** attachment with which all regarded her became while i shared it, my pride and my delite.

Corrected: _____

_____

5. My temper was sometimes violent, and my passions **vehement**; But by some law in my temprature they were turned not towards childish pursuits but to an eager desire to learn, and not to learn all things indiscriminatly.

Corrected: _____

_____

_____

6. I also record those events which led, by insensible steps, too my after tale of misery: For when I would account to myself for the birth of that passion, which afterwards ruled my destiny, I find it arise, like a mountain river, from **ignoble** and almost forgotten sources; but, swelling as it proceded, it became the torrent which, in its course, has swept away all my hopes and joys.

Corrected: _____

_____

_____

_____

_____

_____

7. If, instead of this remark, my father had taken the pains to explane to me that the principles of agrippa had been entirely exploded: and that a modern system of science had been introduced, which possesed much greater powers than the ancient, because the powers of the latter were **chimerical**, while those of the former were real and practical. . . .

Corrected: _____

_____

_____

_____

_____

_____

_____

8. He might dissect anatomize, and give names; But, not to speak of a final cause, causes in their secondery and **tertiary** grades were udderly unknown to him.

Corrected: _____

_____

_____

_____

9. it was a strong effort of the spirit of good; but it was **ineffectuel**

Corrected: _____

_____

Name _____ Period _____

Chapters Three – Five
Note-Taking and Summarizing

Directions: *For Chapters Three through Five, fill in the chart with the necessary information. (Note: Except when writing the summary, you do not need to write in complete sentences.)*

Chapter Three	
Setting	
Characters	
Summary of the Chapter	
Prediction of Coming Events	
Chapter Four	
Setting	
Characters	
Summary of the Chapter	
Prediction of Coming Events	
Chapter Five	
Setting	
Characters	
Summary of the Chapter	
Prediction of Coming Events	

Chapters Three – Five
Comprehension Check

Directions: *To help you understand all aspects of the novel, respond to the following as they relate to Chapters Three through Five. Write your responses on a separate piece of paper using complete sentences.*

Chapter Three

1. Tell what Caroline Frankenstein hopes for Elizabeth and Victor's future.

2. Summarize Elizabeth's response to Caroline's death.

3. Explain why Henry Clerval's father disapproves of education.

4. Deduce what Victor means when he states, "Chance—or rather the evil influence, the Angel of Destruction, which asserted omnipotent sway over me from the moment I turned my reluctant steps from my father's door. . ."

5. Examine how Victor interacts differently with M. Krempe and M. Waldman.

Chapter Four

1. Evaluate Victor's assertion, "In other studies you go as far as others have gone before you, and there is nothing more to know; but in a scientific pursuit there is continual food for discovery and wonder." (48)

2. What specific aspects of biology does Victor study?

3. Explain how Victor thinks that his creation will regard him.

4. Analyze how Victor violates his own advice: "A human being in perfection ought always to preserve a calm and peaceful mind, and never to allow passion or a transitory desire to disturb his tranquility." (53)

5. Generalize why Victor "shuns his fellow-creatures" while working on his creation.

Chapter Five

1. How does Victor react when his creation comes to life? Explain your feelings about his reaction to his creation. Were you surprised? Why or why not?

2. Describe how Victor's dream takes on the mood of a horror story.

3. Show how the passage from Coleridge's "Rime of the Ancient Mariner" applies to Victor Frankenstein. (57)

4. Explain how Victor reacts to Henry Clerval's arrival in Ingolstadt.

5. Surmise what the monster does after leaving Victor's laboratory.

6. Explain the favor that Henry asks of Victor.

Chapters Three – Five
Standards Focus: Literary Archetypes

Literary works frequently pattern themselves after widely-known literature, commonly-held human beliefs or feelings, and historical models. **Archetypes** include a character, setting, theme, or symbol that has a common or recognizable meaning in an entire culture. Archetypes, also called universal symbols, can include colors, themes, familiar characters such as the villain in a black cape, or the young star-crossed lovers, or recurring images such as a snake or a ruined tower. These archetypes add an additional layer of meaning to a novel, and thus, allow the reader to analyze a novel in regards to the emotions and ideas engendered in the archetypes themselves.

Directions: *For each archetype, two passages from Chapters Three through Five have been provided. After reading the passages, explain how the passages exemplify the archetype. Then think of other literary examples for each archetype.*

1. Elizabeth portrays an archetypal virtuous, passive woman.

   On page 41, Shelley describes Elizabeth's reaction to Caroline's death when she states, "She [Elizabeth] veiled her grief, and strove to act the comforter to us all."

   Later, Shelley says about Elizabeth: "She looked steadily on life, and assumed its duties with courage and zeal. She devoted herself to those whom she had been taught to call her uncle and cousins. Never was she so enchanting as at this time when she recalled the sunshine of her smiles and spent them upon us. She forgot even her own regret in her endeavors to make us forget." (41)

   a. Explain how these passages use the archetype of a virtuous, passive woman to portray

      Elizabeth. _____

      _____

      _____

      _____

   b. Individually or as a class, list other stories, poems, movies, or novels that utilize the

      archetype of the virtuous, passive woman. _____

      _____

      _____

2. When Victor strives to creating a living being, he takes on the archetype of a creator god.

   On page 50, Victor states, "After days and nights of incredible labor and fatigue, I succeeded in discovering the cause of generation and life; nay, more, I became myself capable of bestowing animation upon lifeless matter."

   P. 52: "A new species would bless me as its creator and source; many happy and excellent natures would owe their being to me. No father could claim the gratitude of his child so completely as I should deserve theirs."

   a. Explain how these passages use the archetype of a creator god to portray Victor. ____

      _____

_____

_____

b. Individually or as a class, list other stories, poems, movies, or novels that utilize the

archetype of the creator god. _____

_____

_____

3. Victor portrays the archetypal mad scientist in his pursuit to create a living being.

When describing his pursuit, Victor comments on page 49, "Now I was led to examine the cause and progress of this decay, and forced to spend days and nights in vaults and charnel-houses."

P. 52: "One secret which I alone possessed was the hope to which I had dedicated myself; and the moon gazed on my midnight labors, while, with unrelaxed and breathless eagerness, I pursued nature to her hiding-places. Who shall conceive the horrors of my secret toil, as I dabbled among the unhallowed damps of the grave, or tortured the living animal to animate the lifeless clay?"

a. Explain how these passages use the archetype of a mad scientist to portray Victor. __

_____

_____

_____

_____

b. Individually or as a class, list other stories, poems, movies, or novels that utilize the

archetype of the mad scientist. _____

_____

_____

4. Victor Frankenstein's creation has become the archetypal monster of literature and movies.

On page 55, Victor describes the monster's creation when he states, "It was on a dreary night of November that I beheld the accomplishment of my toils. With an anxiety that almost amounted to agony, I collected the instruments of life around me, that I might infuse a spark of being into the lifeless thing that lay at my feet...I saw the dull yellow eye of the creature open; it breathed hard, and a convulsive motion agitated its limbs."

Later, Victor states: ". . . but these luxuriances only formed a more horrid contrast with his watery eyes, that seemed almost of the same color as the dun white sockets in which they were set, his shriveled complexion and straight black lips." (p. 55)

a. Explain how these passages use the archetype of a monster to portray Victor's creation.

_____

_____

_____

_____

_____

b. Individually or as a class, list other stories, poems, movies, or novels that utilize the
    archetype of a monster. _____

_____

_____

_____

c. Discuss how Frankenstein is portrayed in movies and on television. _____

_____

_____

_____

_____

d. What is the common misconception regarding Frankenstein and his monster in terms of
    popular culture, i.e. movies and television? _____

_____

_____

_____

_____

Name _____ Period _____

Chapters Three – Five
Assessment Preparation: Vocabulary in Context

When reading, you must frequently infer the meaning of words by drawing on your knowledge of word roots, examining the **context clues** in the sentence, and noticing how the word is utilized in the sentence.

Directions: *For each bold-faced word, note the word's part of speech and the word's roots. Underline any words in the sentence that provide context clues regarding the meaning of the bold-faced word. Based on the word roots and context clues, infer the word's meaning. Finally, look up the word in a dictionary and write down its meaning.*

Ex. On the third day my mother sickened; her fever was accompanied by the most alarming symptoms, and the <u>looks</u> of her medical attendants **prognosticated** the <u>worst event</u>. (p. 40)

    a. Part of Speech: <u>verb</u>   Word Root: <u>prognosticate</u>

    b. Inference: <u>gave away; showed</u>

    c. Definition: <u>forecasted or predicted</u>

1. It appeared to me sacrilege so soon to leave the **repose**, akin to death, of the house of mourning, and to rush into the thick of life. (41)

    a. Part of Speech: _____ Word Root: _____

    b. Inference: _____

    c. Definition: _____

    _____

2. My life had hitherto been remarkably secluded and domestic; and this had given me invincible **repugnance** to new countenances. (42)

    a. Part of Speech: _____ Word Root: _____

    b. Inference: _____

    c. Definition: _____

    _____

3. I returned home, not disappointed, for I have said that I had long considered those authors useless whom the professor **reprobated**. . ." (43)

    a. Part of Speech: _____ Word Root: _____

    b. Inference: _____

    c. Definition: _____

    _____

4. He began his lecture by a **recapitulation** of the history of chemistry, and the various improvements made by different men of learning, pronouncing with fervor the names of the most distinguished discoverers. (44-45)

    a. Part of Speech: _____ Word Root: _____

    b. Inference: _____

    c. Definition: _____

    _____

5. . . . I expressed myself in measured terms, with the modesty and **deference** due from a youth to his instructor, without letting escape . . . any of the enthusiasm which stimulated my intended labors. (46)

    a. Part of Speech: _____ Word Root: _____

    b. Inference: _____

    c. Definition: _____

    _____

6. His gentleness was never tinged by **dogmatism**; and his instructions were given with an air of frankness and good nature that banished every idea of pedantry. (48)

    a. Part of Speech: _____ Word Root: _____

    b. Inference: _____

    c. Definition: _____

    _____

7. As the minuteness of the parts formed a great **hinderance** to my speed, I resolved, contrary to my first intention, to make the being of a gigantic stature. . ." (51-52)

    a. Part of Speech: _____ Word Root: _____

    b. Inference: _____

    c. Definition: _____

    _____

8. . . . my labors would soon end, and I believed that exercise and amusement would then drive away **incipient** disease; and I promised myself both of these when my creation should be complete. (54)

    a. Part of Speech: _____ Word Root: _____

    b. Inference: _____

    c. Definition: _____

    _____

9. Sometimes my pulse beat so quickly and hardly that I felt the palpitation of every artery; at others, I nearly sank to the ground through **languor** and extreme weakness. (56)

    a. Part of Speech: _____ Word Root: _____

    b. Inference: _____

    c. Definition: _____

    _____

Name _____ Period _____

Chapters Six – Eight
Note-Taking and Summarizing

Directions: For Chapters Six through Eight, fill in the chart with the necessary information. (Note: Except when writing the summary, you do not need to write in complete sentences.)

Chapter Six	
Setting	
Characters	
Summary of the Chapter	
Prediction of Coming Events	
Chapter Seven	
Setting	
Characters	
Summary of the Chapter	
Prediction of Coming Events	
Chapter Eight	
Setting	
Characters	
Summary of the Chapter	
Prediction of Coming Events	

Chapters Six – Eight
Comprehension Check

Directions: *To help you understand all aspects of the novel, respond to the following as they relate to Chapters Six through Eight. Write your responses on a separate piece of paper using complete sentences.*

Chapter Six
1. Summarize Elizabeth's letter to Victor.
2. Relate how Justine comes to live with the Frankenstein family.
3. Visually or descriptively illustrate William Frankenstein.
4. Analyze how Victor feels after he reads Elizabeth's letter.
5. Generalize how M. Waldman and M. Krempe speak of Victor when he and Clerval visit them. What is the irony of this?
6. What do Victor and Clerval begin studying together?
7. Assess how Clerval affects Victor and his mood.

Chapter Seven
1. How does William die?
2. Why does Elizabeth blame herself?
3. How long has it been since Victor has been home?
4. Contrast Victor's feelings about the Swiss landscape during the day with how he views it at night.
5. Examine how the author utilizes the lightning motif as Victor returns home.
6. How does Victor talk himself out of pursuing the beast?
7. Do you believe that Victor could have prevented William's death if he had come home sooner? Why or why not?
8. Explain what Victor mistakenly believes when he tells Ernest, "The murderer discovered! Good God! How can that be? Who could attempt to pursue him? It is impossible; one might as well try to overtake the winds, or confine a mountain stream with straw." (77)
9. Specify the evidence that is used to charge Justine with the crime.
10. Why does Elizabeth refuse to believe that Justine is guilty?

Chapter Eight
1. Tell why Victor does not announce the real murderer, nor confess to the crime himself.
2. Discuss how the evidence against Justine builds.
3. Examine the accuracy of Justine's assertion, "I believe that I have no enemy on earth, and none surely would have been so wicked as to destroy me wantonly." (82)
4. Explain how Elizabeth defends Justine.
5. Why does Victor claim he is suffering worse than the accused?
6. Do you believe that Justine would have been convicted of William's murder if she had not confessed to it? Why or why not?
7. Tell why Justine confesses to William's murder.
8. Evaluate Victor's decision to keep his suspicions regarding William's murder to himself. Do you agree or disagree with the decision he made? Provide details to support your answer.
9. Mary Shelley wrote Chapter Eight as a commentary on what was, in her opinion, a flawed legal system. Provide examples of how Justine may have received an unfair trial.

Chapters Six – Eight
Standards Focus: Imagery

Authors utilize **imagery** to bring a literary work to life. By using descriptive language, an author can paint a picture in the reader's mind. Mary Shelley incorporates numerous examples of imagery when Victor spies his creation while traveling in Switzerland.

Directions: In each box, copy down a minimum of two phrases or sentences from pages 72-75 of Chapter Seven that appeal to the senses of sight, sound, and touch. When you have completed this, look through the text to find examples of Victor comparing his emotions to his surroundings. Be sure to include the page and paragraph number after each quote. An example has been completed for you.

Sight

"I contemplated the lake: the waters were placid; all around was calm; and the snowy mountains, 'the palaces of nature,' were not changed." (p. 73, par. 1)

Sound

Touch

Emotional Response

Utilize the quotes from your chart to write a paragraph explaining how Mary Shelley uses imagery to mirror Victor's mood, as well as to evoke feelings of foreboding in the reader. If you need more room, use a separate piece of paper.

_____

_____

_____

_____

_____

_____

_____

_____

Name _____ Period _____

Chapters Six – Eight
Assessment Preparation: Verb Tense

The **tense of a verb** means the time indicated by it. Verbs typically have 5 basic tenses:

- simple present (They run.)
- present perfect (They have run.)
- simple past (They ran.)
- past perfect (They had run.)
- future (They will run.)
- future perfect (They will have run.)

Directions: *Fill in each blank with the indicated form of selected verb. An example has been completed for you.*

Ex. He ___looks___ (present of "to look") upon study as an odious fetter. . .

1. She _____ (present of "to be") very clever and gentle, and extremely pretty; as I mentioned before, her mien and her expressions continually _____ (present of "to remind") me of my dear aunt.

2. M. Krempe _____ (past of "to be") not equally docile; and in my condition at that time, of almost insupportable sensitiveness, his harsh blunt encomiums _____ (past of "to give") me even more pain than the benevolent approbation of M. Waldman.

3. "I can offer you no consolation, my friend," _____ (past of "to say") he; "your disaster _____ (present of "to be") irreparable. What do you _____ (present of "to intend") to do?"

4. I _____ (past of "to contemplate") the lake: the waters _____ (past of "to be") placid; all around _____ (past of "to be") calm; and the snowy mountains, "the palaces of nature," _____ not _____ (past perfect of "to change").

5. The noble war in the sky _____ (past of "to elevate") my spirits; I _____ (past of "to clasp") my hands, and _____ (past of "to exclaim") aloud, "William, dear angel! this _____ (present of "to be") thy funeral, this thy dirge!"

6. I _____ (past of "to remember") also the nervous fever with which I
    _____ (past perfect of "to seize") just at the time that I dated my
    creation, and which _____ (future of "to give") an air of delirium to a
    tale otherwise so utterly improbable.

7. "We _____ (present of "to do") also, unfortunately," _____ (past of
    "to reply") my father; "for indeed I had rather have been for ever ignorant than
    _____ (present perfect of "to discover") so much depravity and
    ingratitude in one I _____ (past of "to value") so highly."

8. ... but several circumstances came out, that have almost _____ (past of
    "force") conviction upon us; and her own behavior _____ (present
    perfect of "to be") so confused, as to add to the evidence of facts a weight that, I
    fear, _____ (present of " to leave") no hope for doubt. But she
    _____ (future of "to be" tried to-day, and then you _____
    (future of "hear") all.

9. Justine also _____ (past of "to be") a girl of merit, and
    _____ (past of "to possess") qualities which promised to render
    her life happy: now all was to be _____ (past of "to obliterate") in an
    ignominious grave; and I the cause!

Name _____   Period _____

Chapters Nine – Ten
Note-Taking and Summarizing

Directions: *For Chapters Nine and Ten, fill in the chart with the necessary information.*
(Note: Except when writing the summary, you do not need to write in complete sentences.)

Chapter Nine	
Setting	
Characters	
Summary of the Chapter	
Prediction of Coming Events	
Chapter Ten	
Setting	
Characters	
Summary of the Chapter	
Prediction of Coming Events	

Chapters Nine – Ten
Comprehension Check

Directions: *To help you understand all aspects of the novel, respond to the following as they relate to Chapters Nine and Ten. Write your responses on a separate piece of paper using complete sentences.*

Chapter Nine

1. Tell how Victor responds to William's and Justine's deaths.

2. Summarize what Victor does at night after the rest of his family has gone to bed.

3. Show the irony in Victor's desire to "extinguish the life which I [he] had so thoughtlessly bestowed." (90)

4. Explain why Victor feels that he is the "true murderer" of William and Justine.

5. Read the excerpt from Percy Bysshe Shelley's poem "Mont Blanc" on page 50 and compare it to Mary Shelley's narrative description of the region on pages 92-93. Evaluate whether Percy or Mary Shelley provides a better visual picture of the mountain. Provide details from the selections to support your answers.

Chapter Ten

1. Locate a quote that conveys the Romantic belief in nature as a healing force.

2. Compare Shelley's description of the setting to Victor's mood.

3. Examine why Mary Shelley inserts the last stanza of Percy Shelley's "Mutability" into the narrative. (96)

4. Explain how the creature offers an ultimatum to Victor.

5. Generalize how the creature blames humanity for his behavior.

6. What is the creature's chief complaint?

7. How do you feel about the creature now that you have heard him implore Frankenstein to hear his story?

8. Predict what you think the creature wants from Frankenstein.

Excerpt from *Mont Blanc: Lines Written in the Vale of Chamouni* (1817)

by Percy Bysshe Shelley (1792-1822)

1

The everlasting universe of things
Flows through the mind, and rolls its rapid waves,
Now dark – now glittering – now reflecting gloom –
Now lending splendor, where from secret springs
The source of human thought its tribute brings   5
Of waters, —with a sound but half its own,
Such as a feeble brook will oft assume
In the wild woods, among the mountains lone,
Where waterfalls around it leap for ever,
Where woods and winds contend, and a vast river   10
Over its rocks ceaselessly bursts and raves.

2

Thus thou, Ravine of Arve – dark, deep Ravine—
Thou many-colored, many voiced vale,
Over whose pines, and crags, and caverns sail
Fast cloud-shadows and sunbeams: awful scene,   15
Where Power in likeness of the Arve comes down
From the ice-gulfs that gird his secret throne,
Bursting through these dark mountains like the flame
Of lightning through the tempest; —thou dost lie,
Thy giant brood of pines around thee clinging,   20
Children of elder time, in whose devotion
The chainless winds still come and ever came
To drink their odors, and their mighty swinging
To hear – an old and solemn harmony;
Thine earthly rainbows stretched across the sweep   25
Of the ethereal waterfall, whose veil
Robes some unsculptured image; the strange sleep
Which when the voices of the desert fail
Wraps all in its own deep eternity;-
Thy caverns echoing to the Arve's commotion,   30
A loud, lone sound no other sound can tame;
Thou art pervaded with that ceaseless motion,
Thou art the path of that unresting sound—
Dizzy Ravine! and when I gaze on thee
I seem as in a trance sublime and strange   35
To muse on my own separate fantasy,
My own, my human mind, which passively
Now renders and receives fast influencings,
Holding an unremitting interchange
With the clear universe of things around;   40
One legion of wild thoughts, whose wandering wings

Now float above thy darkness, and now rest
Where that or thou art no unbidden guest,
In the still cave of the witch Poesy,
Seeking among the shadows that pass by   45
Ghosts of all things that are, some shade of thee,
Some phantom, some faint image; till the breast
From which they fled recalls them, thou art there!

3

Some say that gleams of a remoter world
Visit the soul in sleep, —that death is slumber,   50
And that its shapes the busy thoughts outnumber
Of those who wake and live. I look on high;
Has some unknown omnipotence unfurled
The veil of life and death? or do I lie
In dream, and does the mightier world of sleep   55
Spread far and round and inaccessibly
Its circles? For the very spirit fails,
Driven like a homeless cloud from steep to steep
That vanishes among the viewless gales!
Far, far above, piercing the infinite sky,   60
Mont Blanc appears, —still snowy and serene—
Its subject mountains their unearthly forms
Pile around it, ice and rock; broad vales between
Of frozen floods, unfathomable deeps,
Blue as the overhanging heaven, that spread   65
And wind among the accumulated steeps;
A desert peopled by the storms alone,
Save when the eagle brings some hunter's bone,
And the wolf tracks her there - how hideously
Its shapes are heaped around! rude, bare, and high,   70
Ghastly, and scarred, and riven. —Is this the scene
Where the old Earthquake-demon taught her young
Ruin? Were these their toys? or did a sea
Of fire envelop once this silent snow?
None can reply—all seems eternal now.   75
The wilderness has a mysterious tongue
Which teaches awful doubt, or faith so mild,
So solemn, so serene, that man may be,
But for such faith, with nature reconciled;
Thou hast a voice, great Mountain, to repeal   80
Large codes of fraud and woe; not understood
By all, but which the wise, and great, and good
Interpret, or make felt, or deeply feel...

Chapters Nine – Ten
Standards Focus: Foreshadowing

An author frequently includes subtle details or clues which hint at, or **foreshadow**, upcoming events in a novel. Foreshadowing allows an author to build a novel while laying the groundwork for upcoming character and plot development. To utilize foreshadowing, an author must plan the entire scope of a novel before he/she begins to write. Detailed planning allows the author to include foreshadowing throughout the novel.

Directions: *Below are some examples of foreshadowing in* **Frankenstein.** *For each example,* **a.** *list the details from the excerpt that indicate possible future events,* **b.** *write a* **specific** *prediction about the character or plot development that you believe is being foreshadowed, then* **c.** *explain* **why** *you believe the text foreshadows your prediction. After you finish reading the novel, you will reread your predictions to see how accurate they were. An example has been completed for you.*

Ex. "But I [Victor] was restrained, when I thought of the heroic and suffering Elizabeth, whom I tenderly loved, and whose existence was bound up in mine. I thought also of my father and surviving brother: should I by my base desertion leave them exposed and unprotected to the malice of the fiend whom I had let loose among them?" (89)

   a. Details that may foreshadow coming events: Elizabeth's existence is connected to Victor's; fiend possibly harming another member of Victor's family
   b. Prediction: The fiend will harm Elizabeth or another member of Victor's family.
   c. Reason for prediction: The fiend has previously demonstrated that he will harm a member of the Frankenstein family to get back at Victor; if Frankenstein does not comply with the creature's demands, he may again lash out.

1. I [Victor] had an obscure feeling that all was not over, and that he [creature] would still commit some signal crime, which by its enormity should almost efface the recollection of the past. (89-90)

   a. Details that may foreshadow coming events: _____

      _____

   b. Prediction: _____

      _____

   c. Reason for prediction: _____

      _____

2. When I [Victor] reflected on his [creature's] crimes and malice, my hatred and revenge burst all bounds of moderation. I would have made a pilgrimage to the highest peak of the Andes, could I, when there, have precipitated him to their base. I

wished to see him again, that I might wreak the utmost extent of abhorrence on his head, and avenge the deaths of William and Justine. (90)

    a. Details that may foreshadow coming events: _____

_____

    b. Prediction: _____

_____

    c. Reason for prediction: _____

_____

3. And could not such words from her whom I [Victor] fondly prized before every other gift of fortune, suffice to chase away the fiend that lurked in my heart? Even as she spoke I drew near to her [Elizabeth], as if in terror; lest at that very moment the destroyer had been near to rob me of her. (91)

    a. Details that may foreshadow coming events: _____

_____

    b. Prediction: _____

_____

    c. Reason for prediction: _____

_____

4. "'You [Victor] purpose to kill me [creature]. How dare you sport thus with life? Do your duty towards me, and I will do mine towards you and the rest of mankind. If you will comply with my conditions, I will leave them and you at peace; but if you refuse, I will glut the maw of death, until it be satiated with the blood of your remaining friends.'" (97)

    a. Details that may foreshadow coming events: _____

_____

    b. Prediction: _____

_____

    c. Reason for prediction: _____

_____

5. "'Life, although it may only be an accumulation of anguish, is dear to me [creature], and I will defend it. Remember, thou [Victor] hast made me more powerful than thyself; my height is superior to thine; my joints more supple. But I will not be tempted to set myself in opposition to thee.'" (97-98)

    a. Details that may foreshadow coming events: _____

_____

   b. Prediction: _____

           _____

   c. Reason for prediction: _____

           _____

6. "I [creature] am miserable, and they [humanity] shall share my wretchedness. Yet it is in your [Victor's] power to recompense me, and deliver them from an evil which it only remains for you to make so great that not only you and your family, but thousands of others, shall be swallowed up in the whirlwinds of rage. Let your compassion be moved, and do not disdain me." (98)

   a. Details that may foreshadow coming events: _____

           _____

   b. Prediction: _____

           _____

   c. Reason for prediction: _____

           _____

7. For the first time, also, I [Victor] felt what the duties of a creator towards his creature were, and that I ought to render him [creature] happy before I complained of his wickedness. (99)

   a. Details that may foreshadow coming events: _____

           _____

   b. Prediction: _____

           _____

   c. Reason for prediction: _____

           _____

Chapters Nine – Ten
Assessment Preparation: Precise Word Choice

Authors carefully select specific words when writing. Utilizing precise vocabulary can subtly adjust and influence the tone, mood, strength, and meaning of a text.

Directions: *Below are excerpts from **Frankenstein** that include precise language. Rewrite each sentence substituting a similar, but less specific word or phrase for the underlined vocabulary word. Then explain why the underlined word more effectively conveys the author's meaning. Use your definitions list or a dictionary for help. An example has been completed for you.*

Ex. "Do you think, Victor," said he [Alphonse Frankenstein], "that I do not suffer also? No one could love a child more than I loved your brother," (tears came into his eyes as he spoke); "but is it not a duty to the survivors, that we should refrain from <u>augmenting</u> their unhappiness by an appearance of immoderate grief?" (88)

    a. Rewritten Sentence: <u>"Do you think, Victor," said he [Alphonse Frankenstein], "that I do not suffer also? No one could love a child more than I loved your brother," (tears came into his eyes as he spoke); "but is it not a duty to the survivors, that we should refrain from adding to their unhappiness by an appearance of immoderate grief?"</u>

    b. Explanation: <u>Augmenting means to enlarge or heighten by any method or amount, not just in number. By using the words "adding to" it sounds as if it is just increased by number. It doesn't give the feeling of an increase in emotion, as the author intended.</u>

1. I thought also of my father and surviving brother: should I by my <u>base</u> desertion leave them exposed and unprotected to the malice of the fiend whom I had let loose among them? (89)

    a. Rewritten Sentence: _____

    _____

    _____

    b. Explanation: _____

    _____

    _____

2. I had an obscure feeling that all was not over, and that he would still commit some signal crime, which by its enormity should almost <u>efface</u> the recollection of the past. (90)

    a. Rewritten Sentence: _____

    _____

    _____

    b. Explanation: _____

    _____

    _____

3. I feel as if I were walking on the edge of a precipice, towards which thousands are crowding, and endeavoring to plunge me into the <u>abyss</u>. (91)

    a. Rewritten Sentence: _____

    _____

    _____

    b. Explanation: _____

    _____

    _____

4. The weather was fine: it was about the middle of the month of August, nearly two months after the death of Justine; that miserable <u>epoch</u> from which I [Victor] dated all my woe. (92)

    a. Rewritten Sentence: _____

    _____

    _____

    b. Explanation: _____

    _____

    _____

5. For a short space of time I remained at the window, watching the <u>pallid</u> lightnings that played above Mont Blanc, and listening to the rushing of the Arve, which pursued its noisy way beneath. (93)

    a. Rewritten Sentence: _____

    _____

    _____

    b. Explanation: _____

    _____

    _____

6. The ascent is <u>precipitous</u>, but the path is cut into continual and short windings, which enable you to surmount the perpendicularity of the mountain. (95)

    a. Rewritten Sentence: _____

    _____

    _____

    b. Explanation: _____

    _____

    _____

7. I perceived, as the shape came nearer (sight tremendous and <u>abhorred</u>!) that it was the
    wretch whom I had created. (96)

    a. Rewritten Sentence: _____

    _____

    _____

    b. Explanation: _____

    _____

    _____

8. "Begone, vile insect! or rather, stay, that I may trample you to dust! and, oh! that I could,
    with the extinction of your miserable existence, restore those victims whom you have so
    <u>diabolically</u> murdered!" (97)

    a. Rewritten Sentence: _____

    _____

    _____

    _____

    b. Explanation: _____

    _____

    _____

9. "Let your compassion be moved, and do not <u>disdain</u> me." (98)

    a. Rewritten Sentence: _____

    _____

    b. Explanation: _____

    _____

    _____

Name _____   Period _____

Chapters Eleven – Twelve
Note-Taking and Summarizing

Directions: For Chapters Eleven and Twelve, fill in the chart with the necessary information. (Note: Except when writing the summary, you do not need to write in complete sentences.)

Chapter Eleven	
Setting	
Characters	
Summary of the Chapter	
Prediction of Coming Events	
Chapter Twelve	
Setting	
Characters	
Summary of the Chapter	
Prediction of Coming Events	

Chapters Eleven – Twelve
Comprehension Check

Directions: *To help you understand all aspects of the novel, respond to the following as they relate to Chapters Eleven and Twelve. Write your responses on a separate piece of paper using complete sentences.*

Chapter Eleven

1. From whose point of view are Chapters Eleven and Twelve told?

2. Summarize the creature's first experiences when he leaves Ingolstadt.

3. Explain how the creature learns about fire.

4. Analyze how the creature is similar to an infant.

5. Generalize what the creature learns about humans from his first encounters with them.

6. Evaluate the creature's decision to isolate himself from humans.

7. Describe the family that the creature observes.

Chapter Twelve

1. Contrast the creature's assessment of the DeLaceys' lifestyle with its reality.

2. Tell how the creature assists the DeLacey family.

3. Calculate how long the creature observes the DeLacey family.

4. Discuss how the creature learns from the family.

5. Explain why the creature wants to learn to speak.

6. Determine the irony in the creature looking upon the DeLaceys as "superior beings." (113)

7. Create a plan for the creature to introduce himself to the DeLaceys. Assess how the DeLaceys would receive the creature.

Name _____ Period _____

Chapters Eleven – Twelve
Standards Focus: Symbolism

In literature, authors frequently use **symbols** to represent meaning in a novel. Just as blooming flowers exemplify spring and changing leaves illustrate fall, an author utilizes **symbolism** to add depth to his/her writing. In *Frankenstein*, Mary Shelley connects several aspects of the text with abstract concepts or ideas, just as changing leaves make a connection with fall.

Throughout the novel, Shelley introduces and expands on the concepts of birth and death. When the creature describes his initial life and feeling sensations for the first time, he roughly follows the order of a biblical creation.

Part One: Biblical Creation
Directions: List the aspects of the creature's development that parallel each item in the process of biblical creation. You may want to refer directly to the text for help.

Aspects of Creation	Parallels in *Frankenstein*
Creation of light	
Creation of earth and seas	
Creation of plants	
Creation of day and night	
Creation of birds and fish	
Creation of human life	

Part Two: Mary Shelley repeatedly utilizes fire and lightning to elucidate Victor's realizations and knowledge.

Directions: For each chapter indicated, locate examples of fire and lightning and explain how Shelly uses each symbolically.

Chapter	Passage	Symbolic Explanation
11		

7		
5		
2		

Part Three: Shelley also utilizes seasons, weather, and nature to symbolize the feelings of Victor and the creature.

Directions: *Locate and explain examples of the seasons, weather, and nature being used symbolically.*

Chapter	Passage	Symbolic Explanation
12		
10		
9		
5		

Directions: On a separate piece of paper, write a paragraph or two explaining how Mary Shelley utilizes the symbolism of creation, fire and lightning, or nature in *Frankenstein*.

Chapters Eleven – Twelve
Assessment Preparation: Complements

Predicate adjectives, predicate nominatives, direct objects, and indirect objects all function as complements.

- A **predicate adjective** follows a *linking verb* and modifies the subject

                                                LV   PA
  Ex. *After staying up too late the previous night, the* <u>child</u> <u>was</u> `sleepy.`

- A **predicate nominative** follows a linking verb and renames or explains the subject.

                            LV   PN
  Ex. *<u>Mary Shelley</u> <u>is</u> the* `author` *of **Frankenstein**.*

- A **direct object** follows an action verb and receives the action from the verb.

                                  AV   DO
  Ex. *<u>Victor Frankenstein</u> <u>built</u> his* `creature` *from body parts.*

- An **indirect object** precedes the direct object and tells to whom/what or for whom/what the action of the verb is done.

                           AV   IO   DO
  Ex. *<u>Sarah</u> <u>gave</u>* `her father a book` *for his birthday.*

Directions: Underline each subject(s) once, each verb(s) twice, and draw a box around each complement. Identify each complement as a predicate adjective (PA), predicate nominative (PN), direct object (DO), indirect object (IO).

                                                           DO
Ex. Before, dark and **opaque** <u>bodies</u> <u>had surrounded</u> `me,` impervious to my touch or sight. . . (101)

1. In this **emigration**, I exceedingly lamented the loss of the fire which I had obtained

    through accident. . .

2. I passed three days in three rambles, and at length discovered the open country.

3. As she walked along, seemingly incommoded by the burden, a young man met her,

    whose countenance expressed a deeper despondence.

4. It was a lovely sight, even to me, poor wretch!

5. The old man had, in the meantime, been **pensive**; but, on the appearance of his companions, he assumed a more cheerful air, and they sat down to eat.

6. The family, after having been thus occupied for a short time, extinguished their lights, and retired, as I **conjectured**, to rest.

7. Nothing could exceed the love and respect which the younger cottagers exhibited towards their **venerable** companion.

8. I was at first unable to solve these questions; but perpetual attention and time explained to me many appearances which were at first **enigmatic**.

9. The pleasant showers and genial warmth of spring greatly altered the aspect of the earth.

10. The light became more and more oppressive to me; and, the heat wearying me as I walked, I sought a place where I could receive shade.

11. No distinct ideas occupied my mind; all was confused.

12. I quickly collected some branches; but they were wet, and would not burn.

13. The silver hair and benevolent countenance of the aged cottager won my reverence, while the gentle manners of the girl enticed my love.

Chapters Thirteen – Fourteen
Note-Taking and Summarizing

Directions: *For Chapters Thirteen and Fourteen, fill in the chart with the necessary information. (Note: Except when writing the summary, you do not need to write in complete sentences.)*

Chapter Thirteen	
Setting	
Characters	
Summary of the Chapter	
Prediction of Coming Events	
Chapter Fourteen	
Setting	
Characters	
Summary of the Chapter	
Prediction of Coming Events	

Chapters Thirteen - Fourteen
Comprehension Check

Directions: *To help you understand all aspects of the novel, respond to the following as they relate to Chapters Thirteen and Fourteen. Write your responses on a separate piece of paper using complete sentences.*

Chapter Thirteen

1. Whose arrival improves Felix's spirits? Predict who this stranger is, why she has come, and why she seems to lift Felix's mood.

2. Describe how Safie's presence facilitates the creature's ability to speak and read.

3. Show how the creature demonstrates his fear of encountering humans.

4. Infer what the creature learns of the human spirit from Volney's *Ruins of Empires*.

5. What else does the creature learn about?

6. How does this knowledge make the creature ponder his place in the universe?

7. Evaluate how the creature's reflections demonstrate his innate humanity.

Chapter Fourteen

1. Describe the De Lacey family's background.

2. Summarize the circumstances that caused the De Lacey's ruin.

3. Discuss how the Turk uses Safie to ensure Felix's assistance.

4. Examine how Safie sought to reject the cultural expectations placed on her.

5. Explain the irony of Safie's father not wanting her to marry Felix, a Christian.

6. While Felix is in Italy courting Safie, what happens to his father and Agatha? Why? What happens to the De Lacey family as a result of Felix's actions?

7. Evaluate if the De Lacey family should or should not have assisted the Turk in his escape. Provide details to support your answer.

8. Compose a letter which Safie writes to her father telling of her intention to marry Felix.

Chapters Thirteen - Fourteen
Standards Focus: Philosophical and Political Approach

Authors frequently create their work in response to an era's political events and current philosophical issues. In 1816, when Mary Shelley began writing *Frankenstein*, Napoleon had recently abdicated the French throne, and the question of women's rights was being vaguely discussed. Mary, however, grew up in a home dominated by her mother, Mary Wollstonecraft, who wrote *A Vindication of the Rights of Women* (1796), one of the first feminist essays.

1. To heighten your knowledge of the era that influenced Mary Shelley, use the Internet or other resources to research and note key political, literary, artistic, philosophical, and scientific events that occurred between 1814 and 1816.

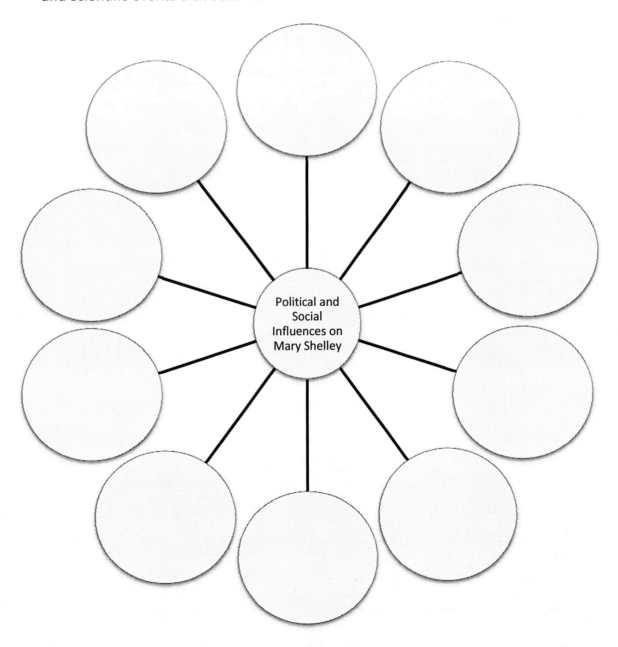

Name _____ Period _____

In *Frankenstein*, Shelley comments on the justice system of the times and conveys a Euro-centric point of view. In light of the historical time period in which it was written, analyze and explain each of the following quotes from the novel.

2. *He [the Turk] was a Turkish merchant, and had inhabited Paris for many years, when, for some reason which I could not learn, he became obnoxious to the government. He was seized and cast into prison the very day that Safie arrived from Constantinople to join him. He was tried and condemned to death. The injustice of his sentence was very flagrant; all Paris was indignant; and it was judged that his religion and wealth, rather than the crime alleged against him, had been the cause of his condemnation.* (121)

   a. According to this quote, why was the Turk convicted? _____

   _____

   _____

   b. How does Shelley use the Turk's story to comment upon the 19th century

   justice systems of Europe? _____

   _____

   _____

   _____

   _____

   _____

   _____

   c. Compare this passage to Shelley's previous condemnation of European

   justice systems. (Think back to Justine's arrest, trial, and conviction.) _____

   _____

   _____

   _____

   _____

Shelley utilizes Safie's story to advance the author's call for women's rights. Explain the following excerpts in light of the author's political desire for women to enjoy more legal rights in Europe.

3. *The young girl spoke in high and enthusiastic terms of her mother, who, born in freedom, spurned the bondage to which she was now reduced. She instructed her daughter in the tenets of her religion, and taught her to aspire to higher powers of intellect, and an independence of spirit, forbidden to the female followers of Mahomet. This lady died; but her lessons were indelibly impressed on the mind of*

Safie, who sickened at the prospect of again returning to Asia and being immured within the walls of a harem, allowed only to occupy herself with infantile amusements, ill suited to the temper of her soul, now accustomed to grand ideas and a noble emulation for virtue. The prospect of marrying a Christian, and remaining in a country where women were allowed to take a rank in society, was enchanting to her. (123)

a. According to this quote, why does Safie scorn the idea of being in a harem?

_____

_____

_____

_____

_____

b. Even though Shelley sets Safie's story against an Arab harem, how could she be utilizing the description to also comment on the position of European (Christian) women of her day? _____

_____

_____

_____

_____

_____

_____

4. Relate how Safie's decisions allow Shelley to demonstrate how women could exercise their rights, even in Shelley's time. _____

_____

_____

_____

_____

_____

_____

Chapters Thirteen - Fourteen
Assessment Preparation: Word Origins—Etymology

Directions: *For each of your vocabulary words from Chapters 13-14:*
   a. *Read the origin of the word and a sentence from the text containing it.*
   b. *Circle the best definition of the word.*
   c. *Write a sentence using the word with its correct definition.*
   d. *List 1-3 more words that have the same Latin, Greek, or Anglo-Saxon root. You may use a reference resource such as a dictionary to find other words.*

An example has been done for you.

Ex. verdure
   a. Word Origin: Middle English < Middle French *verd* "green"; *It surprised me that what before was desert and gloomy should now bloom with the most beautiful flowers and **verdure**.* (115)
   b. Definition: a. baby forest animals; b. green vegetation and plants; c. fallen trees; d. dying weeds
   c. Sentence: While hiking, the couple admired the ferns and other verdure on the forest floor.
   d. Other words: verdant, verdancy, verde

1. dissipates

   a. Word Origin: <Latin *dissipare* "to scatter"; *They made many signs which I did not comprehend; but I saw that her presence diffused gladness through the cottage, dispelling their sorrow as the sun **dissipates** the morning mists.* (116)

   b. Definition: a. scatters in various directions; b. gathers; c. shines brightly; d. glows

   c. Sentence: _____

   _____

   d. Other Words: _____

2. cadence

   a. Word Origin: <Old Italian *cadenza* "ornamental passage near the close of a song"; *She sang, and her voice flowed in a rich **cadence**, swelling or dying away, like a nightingale of the woods.* (117)

   b. Definition: a. throbbing sound; b. celebratory march; c. yell or call for help; d. rhythmic flow of sounds or words

   c. Sentence: _____

   _____

   d. Other Words: _____

3. scion

    a. Word Origin: <Middle English< Old French *cion* "to sprout"; *He appeared at one time a mere **scion** of the evil principle, and at another as all that can be conceived of noble and godlike.* (118)

    b. Definition: a. budding plant; b. descendant or offshoot; c. transplant; d. representative sample

    c. Sentence: _____

    _____

    d. Other Words: _____

4. vagabond

    a. Word Origin: <Latin *vagabundus* "wandering; vagrant"; *A man might be respected with only one of these advantages; but, without either, he was considered, except in very rare instances, as a **vagabond** and a slave, doomed to waste his powers for the profits of the chosen few!* (118-119)

    b. Definition: a. untrustworthy person; b. evil minion; c. competitor; d. person who wanders from place to place

    c. Sentence: _____

    _____

    d. Other Words: _____

5. tenets

    a. Word Origin: <Medieval Latin *tenere* "to hold"; *She instructed her daughter in the **tenets** of her religion, and taught her to aspire to higher powers of intellect, and an independence of spirit, forbidden to the female followers of Mahomet.* (123)

    b. Definition: a. problems; b. moments; c. arguments; d. doctrines

    c. Sentence: _____

    _____

    d. Other Words: _____

6. immured

    a. Word Origin: <Medieval Latin *immurare* < in + *murus* "wall"; *This lady died; but her lessons were indelibly impressed on the mind of Safie, who sickened at the prospect of again returning to Asia and being **immured** within the walls of a harem, allowed only to occupy herself with infantile amusements, ill suited to the temper of her soul, now accustomed to grand ideas and a noble emulation for virtue.* (123)

    b. Definition: a. buried in a shrine; b. shrouded; c. confined; d. revered

    c. Sentence: _____

    _____

    d. Other Words: _____

7. noisome

    a. Word Origin: <Middle English *noie* "harm," <Middle French *anoier* "to annoy"; *His blind and aged father, and his gentle sister, lay in a* **noisome** *dungeon, while he enjoyed the free air and the society of her whom he loved.* (124)

    b. Definition: a. painful; b. offensive; c. noisy; d. freezing

    c. Sentence: _____

    _____

    d. Other Words: _____

8. expostulate

    a. Word Origin: <Latin *expostulare* "to demand"; *The generous nature of Safie was outraged by this command; she attempted to* **expostulate** *with her father, but he left her angrily, reiterating his tyrannical mandate.* (125)

    b. Definition: a. reason earnestly with someone; b. argue; c. share; d. give a speech

    c. Sentence: _____

    _____

    d. Other Words: _____

9. pittance

    a. Word Origin: < Middle English *pitance*, <Old French, "allowance of food to a monk or poor person"; *Felix soon learned that the treacherous Turk, for whom he and his family endured such unheard-of oppression, on discovering that his deliverer was thus reduced to poverty and sending Felix a* **pittance** *of money, to aid him, as he said, in some plan of future maintenance.* (124-125)

    b. Definition: a. large amount; b. collection of coins; c. small amount; d. a loan

    c. Sentence: _____

    _____

    d. Other Words: _____

Name _____ Period _____

Chapters Fifteen – Seventeen
Note-Taking and Summarizing

Directions: For Chapters Fifteen through Seventeen, fill in the chart with the necessary information. (Note: Except when writing the summary, you do not need to write in complete sentences.)

Chapter Fifteen	
Setting	
Characters	
Summary of the Chapter	
Prediction of Coming Events	
Chapter Sixteen	
Setting	
Characters	
Summary of the Chapter	
Prediction of Coming Events	
Chapter Seventeen	
Setting	
Characters	
Summary of the Chapter	
Prediction of Coming Events	

Chapters Fifteen – Seventeen
Comprehension Check

Directions: *To help you understand all aspects of the novel, respond to the following as they relate to Chapters Fifteen through Seventeen. Write your responses on a separate piece of paper using complete sentences.*

Chapter Fifteen

1. Contrast how the creature feels when reading *The Sorrows of Werter* and *Plutarch's Lives*.
2. Examine how the creature sees himself as different from Adam in *Paradise Lost*.
3. Explain how knowledge heightens the creature's frustration with his situation.
4. Generalize how the creature thinks the DeLacey family will respond to his advances.
5. Tell what occurs when the creature meets the DeLacey family.
6. Evaluate the approach the creature takes to introduce himself to the DeLacey family. Would the creature have improved his chances of being accepted by the family if he had done anything differently? If so, what could have helped?

Chapter Sixteen

1. Quote the passage when the creature experiences a turning point in his relationship with humans. What is your reaction to his statement? How do you think the creature will change from this moment of insight?
2. After much thought, how does the creature believe he should have done things differently? What does the creature decide to do?
3. Tell about what the creature sees the next morning, and what he decides to do as a result.
4. Explain why the creature wants to meet Victor.
5. How does the incident with the DeLacey family change the creature?
6. Summarize the creature's encounter with the drowning girl. How does this incident further fuel the creature's hatred for mankind and need for revenge?
7. Describe why the creature chooses to kill William.
8. Tell why the creature places the locket in Justine's pocket.
9. Describe the demand the creature makes of Victor.

Chapter Seventeen

1. Tell how Victor first responds to the creature's demand.
2. Discuss how the creature convinces Victor to make him a mate.
3. Examine how the creature believes companionship will help his temperament.
4. Explain how the creature plans to stay abreast of Victor's progress.
5. Compare the creature's feelings to those of Captain Robert Walton at the beginning of the novel.
6. Recommend whether Victor should or should not create a mate for the creature. What are the advantages; what are the drawbacks?

Chapters Fifteen - Seventeen
Standards Focus: Point of View

Point of view encompasses the viewpoint, or perspective, from which a story is told. The point of view influences how a reader understands a story and how he/she reacts to the characters and their actions.

A novel may be told from the point of view of one of a book's characters, several different characters throughout the book, or from the point of view of a narrator who is not part of the novel. The author can also use point of view to his advantage to elicit from the reader sympathy or other emotional response to a character or characters.

In *Frankenstein*, Mary Shelley allows several characters to take turns telling their stories from their own points of view. Robert Walton's letters frame Victor and the creature's stories through the eyes of the sea captain. Victor Frankenstein's point of view captures his horror regarding the creature's actions, and the creature sheds light on his desires and reasoning process when he tells his own story to Victor.

Directions: Use your knowledge of the novel to complete the following graphic organizers and questions. Include specific details from the text in your answers.

1. By allowing the creature to relate his story from his point of view, Mary Shelley paints the monster as a being with human emotions and desires. Complete the graphic organizer with details from Chapter Fifteen that create sympathy in the reader towards the creature. Two examples have been done for you.

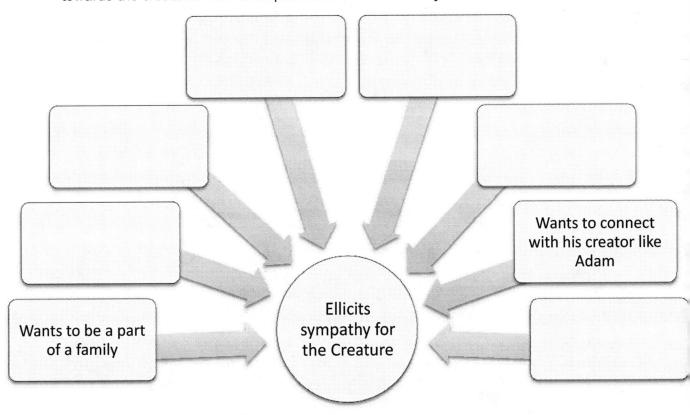

2. Reflect on how you felt when reading about the creature's visit with the DeLacey father and then when Felix beats the creature. Include how the author's use of point of view elicits sympathy for the creature and his situation.

    _____

    _____

    _____

    _____

    _____

    _____

3. When the creature tells Victor about killing William and framing Justine for the murder, the reader gains a glimpse into the crime from a different perspective. Use the Venn diagram below to compare and contrast Victor's previous conception of the crime with the creature's version of it.

Victor's Conception of Crime   Similarities in stories   Creature's version of Crime

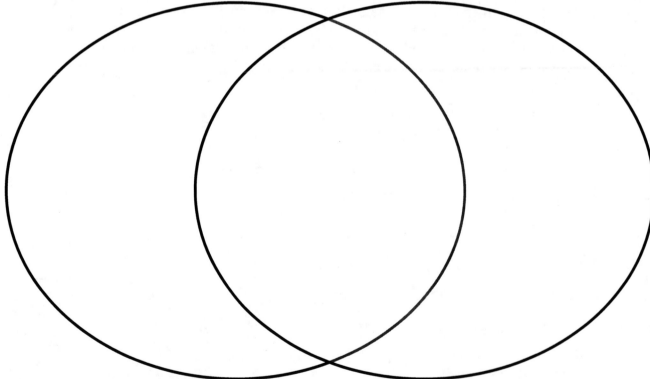

4. Based on the creature's version of his life up to the point where he meets Victor, write an essay judging his reliability as a narrator. Include aspects of his story that you believe and aspects that you find less believable or reliable. Explain why you do or do not believe these details of the creature's story, integrating the text for support.

Chapters Fifteen - Seventeen
Standards Focus: Clauses

A **clause** is a group of words in a sentence that includes a subject and a verb. An **independent clause** can stand alone as a sentence since it expresses a complete thought. A **subordinate or dependent clause** cannot stand alone as a sentence since it does not express a complete thought.

- A dependent **adjective clause** modifies a noun or pronoun. Adjective clauses are introduced by *relatives* such as *who, whose, whom, which, that, whoever, whatever, etc.*
- A dependent **adverb clause** modifies a verb, an adjective, or an adverb. Adverb clauses are introduced by **subordinating conjunctions** such as *after, although, as, as if, as much as, as long as, as soon as, because, before, if, in order that, since, so, that, than, though, unless, until, when, whenever, where, wherever, why,* and *while.*
- *It is important to note that all adjective and adverb clauses are dependent clauses.*

Directions:
(1) For each sentence, underline each subject once and each verb twice.
(2) Place parentheses around each dependent clause.
(3) Circle the relative or subordinating conjunction that accompanies each dependent clause.
(4) Label each dependent clause as an adjective or adverb clause.
   (The vocabulary words used in this exercise appear in bold print.)

                                        Adj. clause
Ex. I learned, from the views of social life (which it developed), to admire their virtues,

and to **deprecate** the vices of mankind.

1. I resolved, at least, not to despair, but in every way to fit myself for an interview with

   them which would decide my fate.

2. I did not pretend to enter into the merits of the case, yet I inclined towards the

   opinions of the hero, whose extinction I wept, without precisely understanding it.

3. I saw him on the point of repeating his blow, when, overcome by pain and anguish, I

   quitted the cottage and in the general tumult escaped unperceived to my hovel.

4. Why, in that instant, did I not extinguish the spark of existence which you had so

   wantonly bestowed?

5. When my hunger was appeased, I directed my steps towards the well-known path

   that conducted to the cottage.

6. As night advanced, I placed a variety of combustibles around the cottage; and, after

   having destroyed every **vestige** of cultivation in the garden, I waited with forced

   impatience until the moon had sunk to commence my operations.

7. From you only could I hope for **succor**, although towards you I felt no sentiment but

   that of hatred.

8. It was late in autumn when I quitted the district where I had so long resided.

9. The child still struggled, and loaded me with **epithets** which carried despair to my

   heart; I grasped his throat to silence him, and in a moment he lay dead at my feet.

10. While I was overcome by these feelings, I left the spot where I had committed the

    murder, and seeking a more secluded hiding-place, I entered a barn which had

    appeared to me to be empty.

11. Shall I respect man when he **contemns** me?

Chapters Eighteen – Twenty
Note-Taking and Summarizing

Directions: *For Chapters Eighteen through Twenty, fill in the chart with the necessary information. (Note: Except when writing the summary, you do not need to write in complete sentences.)*

Chapter Eighteen	
Setting	
Characters	
Summary of the Chapter	
Prediction of Coming Events	
Chapter Nineteen	
Setting	
Characters	
Summary of the Chapter	
Prediction of Coming Events	
Chapter Twenty	
Setting	
Characters	
Summary of the Chapter	
Prediction of Coming Events	

Chapters Eighteen – Twenty
Comprehension Check

Directions: *To help you understand all aspects of the novel, respond to the following as they relate to Chapters Eighteen through Twenty. Write your responses on a separate piece of paper using complete sentences.*

Chapter Eighteen
1. Tell why Alphonse Frankenstein thinks Victor is depressed.
2. Summarize why Victor feels that he cannot marry Elizabeth at this time.
3. Demonstrate how Victor manipulates his father so he has the time and liberty to create a female creature.
4. Analyze why Victor feels that his family will be safer if he leaves Switzerland.
5. Generalize how the setting and scenery of his journey finally affect Victor's mind and spirits.
6. Assess how Victor feels about Clerval's friendship and companionship.

Chapter Nineteen
1. Quote the passage(s) that tells how Victor views his life in regards to the monster and his demand.
2. While Clerval and Victor are in London, how does Clerval occupy his time?
3. Describe how Victor views the process of creating a female creature.
4. To what is Shelley alluding in Victor's assertion: "But I am a blasted tree; the bolt has entered my soul; and I felt then that I should survive to exhibit what I shall soon cease to be—a miserable spectacle of wrecked humanity, pitiable to others, and intolerable to myself"? What does Victor mean?
5. Detail why Victor cannot bear to hear Henry speak of Chamounix.
6. Explain why Victor sometimes fears for Henry's life while on their journey.
7. What does Victor ask of Henry? What does Victor wish to do on his own?
8. Formulate how Victor's selection of the Orkney Islands mirrors his feelings about the task he plans to complete there.
9. Judge Victor's emotional state as he begins to create a female monster.

Chapter Twenty
1. What are Victor's concerns about creating another monster?
2. Explain why Victor destroys the creature he is forming.
3. Examine how the creature conveys the power he believes he has over Victor.
4. Infer what the monster means when he tells Victor, "I shall be with you on your wedding-night."
5. Generalize how Victor feels after the monster threatens him.
6. Evaluate Victor's decision not to create a female monster. Do you think he is making the right decision? Why or why not?
7. What does Victor do with the remains of the female creature?
8. Describe what Victor does when he becomes tired while sailing.
9. Predict why the people in the village think Victor is responsible for the death of a gentleman in the town.

Name _____   Period _____

Chapters Eighteen - Twenty
Standards Focus: Characterization

An author reveals information about a novel's **characters** in a variety of ways. In **direct characterization**, the author directly informs the reader about the character without allowing the reader to infer any information of his own. **Indirect characterization** provides information about the character, but also allows the reader to draw conclusions about the character. Information may be conveyed by describing a characters actions, thoughts, or feelings, as well as observing his/her interactions with other characters.

Directions: Using the clues, locate specific portions of the novel from Chapters Eighteen-Twenty that convey information about Victor Frankenstein. Also categorize each example as direct or indirect characterization and explain what it tells the reader about the characters. An example has been done for you. Once you have completed the chart, write a 2-3 paragraph sketch on the character of Victor Frankenstein at this point in the novel.

Ex. Victor feels torn between creating or not creating a female monster.	
Quote from novel	p. 149; ". . . I could not collect the courage to recommence my work. I feared the vengeance of the disappointed fiend, yet I was unable to overcome my repugnance to the task which was enjoined me. . . I clung to every pretense of delay, and shrunk from taking the first step in an undertaking whose immediate necessity began to appear less absolute to me."
Type of Characterization	Direct characterization
What quote tells the reader about Victor	Victor does not want to create a female monster and only agrees to do so because he fears the male monster and what he might do.

1. Victor is concerned about the safety of his family and friends.	
Quote from novel	
Type of Characterization	
What quote tells the reader about Victor	

2. Victor contrasts his personality before and after creating the male monster.	
Quote from novel	
Type of Characterization	
What quote tells the reader about Victor	

3. Victor loathes the task of creating another monster.	
Quote from novel	
Type of Characterization	
What quote tells the reader about Victor	

4. Victor refuses to create another monster who may do harm.	
Quote from novel	
Type of Characterization	
What quote tells the reader about Victor	

5. Victor struggles with his decision not to create a female monster.	
Quote from novel	
Type of Characterization	
What quote tells the reader about Victor	

Chapters Eighteen - Twenty
Assessment Preparation: Base Words/Root Words/Affixes

To discern the meaning of unfamiliar words, it is helpful to break the word into its base word, root word, and any affixes it may have.

Directions: Look up the vocabulary words from Chapters Eighteen—Twenty in a dictionary. Locate each word's base, root and meaning, any prefixes or suffixes, and definition. Finally, write a sentence using the vocabulary word in its correct context. An example has been done for you.

Example: enjoined

    a. Base Word: _enjoin_   b. Affix(es): _-ed_

    c. Word Root and Meaning: _injungere- to fasten to; bring upon_____

    d. Definition: _verb; directed or ordered to do something_____

    e. Sentence: _His mother enjoined him to clean his room._____

1. enfranchised

    a. Base Word: _____   b. Affix(es): _____

    c. Word Root and Meaning: _____

    d. Definition: _____

    e. Sentence: _____

    _____

2. sedulous

    a. Base Word: _____   b. Affix(es): _____

    c. Word Root and Meaning: _____

    d. Definition: _____

    e. Sentence: _____

    _____

3. variegated

    a. Base Word: _____   b. Affix(es): _____

    c. Word Root and Meaning: _____

    d. Definition: _____

    e. Sentence: _____

    _____

4. eminently

    a. Base Word: _____   b. Affix(es): _____

    c. Word Root and Meaning: _____

    d. Definition: _____

    e. Sentence: _____

    _____

5. **blight**

    a. Base Word: _____   b. Affix(es): _____

    c. Word Root and Meaning: _____

    d. Definition: _____

    e. Sentence: _____

    _____

6. **precarious**

    a. Base Word: _____   b. Affix(es): _____

    c. Word Root and Meaning: _____

    d. Definition: _____

    e. Sentence: _____

    _____

7. **profundity**

    a. Base Word: _____   b. Affix(es): _____

    c. Word Root and Meaning: _____

    d. Definition: _____

    e. Sentence: _____

    _____

8. **impotence**

    a. Base Word: _____   b. Affix(es): _____

    c. Word Root and Meaning: _____

    d. Definition: _____

    e. Sentence: _____

    _____

9. **inexorable**

    a. Base Word: _____   b. Affix(es): _____

    c. Word Root and Meaning: _____

    d. Definition: _____

    e. Sentence: _____

    _____

Name _____ Period _____

Chapters Twenty-One – Twenty-Three
Note-Taking and Summarizing

Directions: For Chapters Twenty-One through Twenty-Three, fill in the chart with the necessary information. (Note: Except when writing the summary, you do not need to write in complete sentences.)

Chapter Twenty-One	
Setting	
Characters	
Summary of the Chapter	
Prediction of Coming Events	
Chapter Twenty-Two	
Setting	
Characters	
Summary of the Chapter	
Prediction of Coming Events	
Chapter Twenty-Three	
Setting	
Characters	
Summary of the Chapter	
Prediction of Coming Events	

Chapters Twenty-One – Twenty-Three
Comprehension Check

Directions: *To help you understand all aspects of the novel, respond to the following as they relate to Chapters Twenty-One through Twenty-Three. Write your answers on a separate piece of paper using complete sentences.*

Chapter Twenty-One
1. How does the dead body's appearance relate its cause of death?
2. Summarize why the townspeople think Victor is the murderer.
3. Who has been murdered?
4. Show how Victor responds to Clerval's death upon seeing his body and how he behaves while in jail.
5. Explain how Mr. Kirwin helps Victor.
6. Formulate what "destiny of the most horrible kind" Victor thinks "hangs over" him. (179)
7. Explain how Victor is acquitted of Clerval's murder. How long was Victor incarcerated?
8. Discuss Victor's emotional response to his acquittal.

Chapter Twenty-Two
1. Examine Victor's assertion, "William, Justine, and Henry—they all died by my hands." (183)
2. Discuss the meaning of Victor telling his father, "A thousand times would I have shed my own blood, drop by drop, to have saved their lives; but I could not, my father, indeed I could not sacrifice the whole human race." (184)
3. Show why Elizabeth thinks Victor is depressed and troubled.
4. Infer what Victor thinks will occur between him and the monster on his wedding-night. What other outcomes does Victor fail to consider?
5. Devise a plan for Victor to tell Elizabeth about the monster.
6. Predict what Victor foreshadows in his comment, "But, as if possessed of magic powers, the monster had blinded me to his real intentions; and when I thought that I had prepared only my own death, I hastened that of a far dearer victim." (189)
7. Tell how Victor tries to protect himself from the monster.

Chapter Twenty-Three
1. How does Shelley utilize nature to foreshadow ominous happenings at the beginning of this chapter?
2. Describe how the monster is with Victor on his wedding-night.
3. Show how Elizabeth's death intensifies Victor's concern for his other loved ones.
4. How does the creature inadvertently kill Alphonse Frankenstein?
5. Formulate how Elizabeth and Alphonse's deaths change Victor's focus in life.
6. Explain why the magistrate does not think that he can offer much help to Victor.
7. Assess how Victor's comment that the creature "may be hunted like the chamois, and destroyed as a beast of prey" relates to his perception of his creation.
8. What is ironic about Victor's statement: "...how ignorant are thou in thy pride of wisdom"?

Chapters Twenty-One – Twenty-Three
Standards Focus: Historical Themes and Issues

Authors construct their work through the lens of the time in which they live. Major themes and issues of the day frequently appear intentionally or unintentionally throughout an author's work. When *Frankenstein* was written in the early nineteenth century, women's issues were just beginning to be raised in society. Mary Shelley's mother Mary Wollstonecraft authored one of the first feminist texts, *A Vindication of the Rights of Women*, in 1796, and Shelley herself exhibited a less than traditional lifestyle when she began a relationship with a married Percy Bysshe Shelley. For all this, it is surprising then that Shelley populates her novel with passive female characters who silently and submissively allow life to happen around them.

Part One
Directions: *Use the clues to locate and analyze specific information regarding the character of Elizabeth Lavenza.*

Looking back through Chapters Twenty-One – Twenty-Three, locate examples of Elizabeth Lavenza's characterization based on her own words or actions or the words or actions of other characters. An example has been done for you.

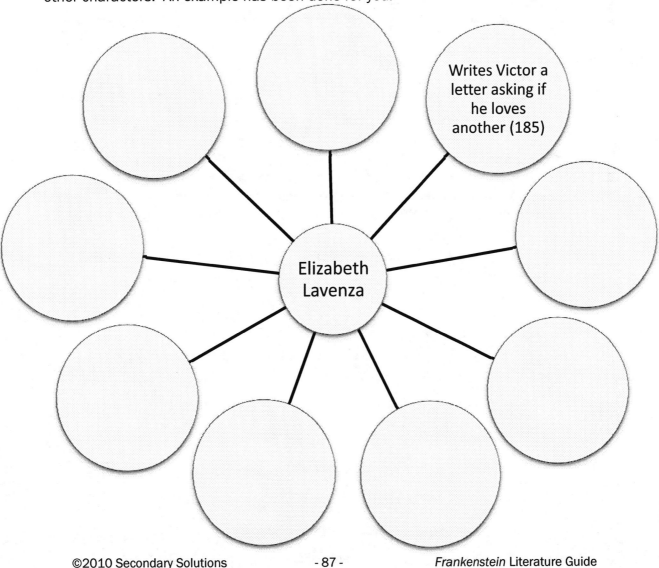

Name _____ Period _____

Part Two
Directions: *Answer the following questions fully on a separate sheet of paper. Staple your answers to your work in Part One.*

_____ 1. Throughout the novel, Elizabeth writes Victor several letters inquiring of his emotional state, as well as his feelings about her. In Chapter Twenty-Two, Elizabeth asks Victor, "Tell me, dearest Victor. Answer me, I conjure you, by our mutual happiness, with simple truth – Do you not love another?" Consider how Elizabeth's letters reflect on her personality and life experiences. How might the dynamic between Elizabeth and Victor be typical of the time period in which the novel was written?

_____ 2. Victor plans to tell Elizabeth about the monster after they are married. Telling Elizabeth of his secret, Victor implores her, "But until then, I conjure you, do not mention or allude to it. This I most earnestly entreat, and I know you will comply." (187)

    a. What does Victor's choice of the word "comply" convey about his relationship with Elizabeth?

    b. Imagine if you were engaged and your prospective spouse noted that he/she would tell you his/her deepest secret after you were married and you were not to ask about it until then. Share how you would feel and what you would do about this request.

_____ 3. After the creature tells Victor that he will be with him on his wedding-night, Victor assumes that the creature will kill him. Provide two points regarding Elizabeth that Victor does not consider while pondering his own death.

_____ 4. After the deaths of William, Justine, and Clerval, Victor collapses into sickness and does not attempt to destroy the monster. Elizabeth's death, however, prompts Victor to confess, "My revenge is of no moment to you; yet, while I allow it to be a vice, I confess that it is the devouring and only passion of my soul." (198) Why do you think Victor responds to Elizabeth's death differently than he does to the previous deaths?

_____ 5. On a separate piece of paper, write an essay discussing the portrayal of women in *Frankenstein*.

Chapters Twenty-One – Twenty-Three
Assessment Preparation: Sentence Structure

An **independent clause** expresses a complete thought and can stand alone as a sentence. A **dependent or subordinate clause** does not express a complete thought and cannot stand alone as sentence.

- A **simple sentence** contains one independent clause and no dependent clauses.
- A **compound sentence** contains two or more independent clauses, but no dependent clauses.
- A **complex sentence** contains one independent clause and one or more dependent clauses.
- A **compound-complex sentence** contains two or more independent clauses and one or more dependent clauses.

Directions: *For each sentence, underline each <u>subject</u> once and each <u>verb</u> twice. Place [brackets] around each dependent clause. Finally, identify each sentence as simple, compound, complex, or compound-complex. (Your vocabulary words are in bold print.)*

Ex. Their first **supposition** <u>was</u> [that <u>it</u> <u>was</u> the corpse of some person] [<u>who</u> <u>had been</u> <u>drowned</u>, and <u>was thrown</u> on shore by the waves]; but, on examination, <u>they</u> <u>found</u> [that the <u>clothes</u> <u>were</u> not wet], and even [that the <u>body</u> <u>was</u> not then cold].

Type of sentence: <u>compound-complex sentence</u>

1. I turned with loathing from the woman who could utter so unfeeling a speech to a person just saved, on the very edge of death; but I felt **languid**, and unable to reflect on all that had passed.

   Type of sentence: _____

2. The physician came and prescribed medicines, and the old woman prepared them for me; but utter carelessness was visible in the first, and the expression of brutality was strongly marked in the **visage** of the second.

   Type of sentence: _____

3. My father was enraptured on finding me freed from the **vexations** of a criminal

    charge, that I was again allowed to breathe the fresh atmosphere, and permitted to

    return to my native country.

    Type of sentence: _____

4. Sometimes he thought that I felt deeply the **degradation** of being obliged to answer a

    charge of murder, and he endeavored to prove to me the futility of pride.

    Type of sentence: _____

5. By the utmost self-violence, I curbed the **imperious** voice of wretchedness, which

    sometimes desired to declare itself to the whole world; and my manners were calmer

    and more composed than they had ever been since my journey to the sea of ice.

    Type of sentence: _____

6. If he were **vanquished** I should be a free man!

    Type of sentence: _____

7. He had vowed to be with me on my wedding-night, yet he did not consider that threat

    as binding him to peace in the meantime; for, as if to show me that he was not yet

    satiated with blood, he had murdered Clerval immediately after the **enunciation** of his

    threats.

    Type of sentence: _____

8. I carried pistols and a dagger constantly about me, and was ever on the watch to

    prevent **artifice**; and by these means gained a greater degree of tranquility.

    Type of sentence: _____

9. But her temper was fluctuating; joy for a few instants shone in her eyes, but it

    continually gave place to distraction and **reverie**.

    Type of sentence: _____

Name _____   Period _____

Chapters Twenty-Four - Continuation
Note-Taking and Summarizing

Directions: *For Chapter **Twenty-Four through the Continuation of Walton's letters,** fill in the chart with the necessary information. (Note: Except when writing the summary, you do not need to write in complete sentences.)*

Chapter Twenty-Four	
Setting	
Characters	
Summary of the Chapter	
Prediction of Coming Events	
Continuation	
Setting	
Characters	
Summary of the Letters	

Chapters Twenty-Four – Continuation
Comprehension Check

Directions: To help you understand all aspects of the novel, respond to the following as they relate to Chapters Twenty-Four through Continuation. Write your responses on a separate piece of paper using complete sentences.

Chapter Twenty-Four

1. Tell where Victor travels. Where is he going, and why?

2. How does Victor feel as if he is being guided by a "spirit of good"?

3. Describe how Victor and the creature's roles have reversed.

4. Point out why the creature leaves Victor hints and marks regarding his trail.

5. Infer the creature's meaning when he tells Victor, "My reign is not yet over. . . you live, and my power is complete." (202)

6. Generalize the creature's state of mind and how he views humans while on his journey.

7. Evaluate Victor's sanity and ability to make rational decisions as he pursues the creature.

8. What natural event threatens Victor's safety?

9. Interpret Victor's thoughts when he repeatedly refers to "guiding spirits."

Continuation

1. Why are Felix and Safie's letters important to Walton?

2. Summarize the situation aboard Walton's ship.

3. Relate how Walton has spent most of his time since Victor boarded the ship.

4. Summarize Frankenstein's speech to the crew.

5. How does Victor's speech parallel his quest for the creature?

6. Analyze why Walton decides to take the ship south.

7. Assess Victor's statement, "In a fit of enthusiastic madness I created a rational creature, and was bound toward him, to assure, as far as was in my power, his happiness and well-being." (214) Why is this statement surprising?

8. If Victor had not died, what do you think he would have done?

9. Who does Walton find with Victor?

10. Discuss how the monster feels now that Victor is dead.

11. Examine the creature's belief, "I was the slave, not the master, of an impulse which I detested, yet could not disobey." (217)

12. Infer why the creature leaves Walton's ship.

Chapters Twenty-Four – Continuation
Standards Focus: Themes

Themes are the key ideas in a work of literature. While a novel may evoke a variety of ideas, the work's themes constantly reappear and extend throughout the piece of literature. To support a theme, the author revisits and supports the idea with textual evidence throughout the novel.

Shelley introduces the themes of using knowledge for good or evil purposes, desire for companionship, and the power of nature at the beginning of the novel and continues them throughout the text.

Directions: *Complete the graphic organizers with specific instances of each theme as it arises in the novel. You may use examples from throughout the entire book. An example for each has been completed for you.*

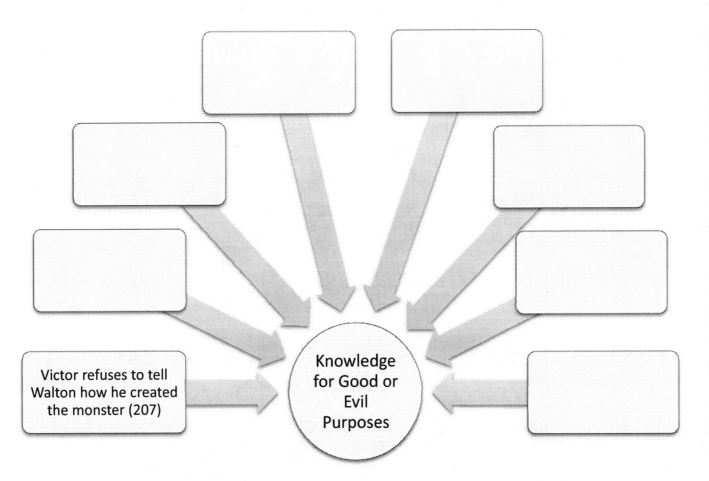

Victor refuses to tell Walton how he created the monster (207)

Knowledge for Good or Evil Purposes

Name _____   Period _____

The Desire for
Companionship

Walton comments on
his desire for a friend
(208)

The Power of
Nature

The breaking ice floes
threaten Victor's quest
(205)

Name _____   Period _____

Chapters Twenty-Four – Continuation
Assessment Preparation: Analogies

An analogy is a shortened way of stating the relationship between a word and an idea. One type of analogy expresses the relationship between synonyms. Below is an example:

      rare : scarce :: abundant : plentiful

This means that the relationship between *rare* and *scarce* is the same as the relationship between *abundant* and *plentiful*. (The symbol " : " means "is to" and the symbol " :: " means "as"). An analogy may also involve antonyms. For example:

      narrow : wide :: long : short

Another way to state this analogy is: "*narrow* is to *wide* as *long* is to *short*."

There are other types of analogies. The word pairs in an analogy could also be:
- **descriptive**, in which one word describes the other word, as in GREEN : GRASS
- **part to whole**, in which one word is a part or piece of the other, as in TOE : FOOT
- **item to category**, in which one word names something that falls into the group named by the other word, as in CARROT : VEGETABLE

Directions: To help you when completing the analogy, first identify the relationship between the first pair of words in the analogy. Then using a thesaurus and/or a dictionary, select the best word from the list below to complete the analogy. An example has been done for you.

repast	scoffing	procured	disencumbered
congeal	disposition	actuated	superfluous
contumely	~~abjuration~~		

Ex. indulge : withhold :: defiance : ____abjuration____
Relationship: Indulge and withhold, as well as defiance and abjuration, are antonyms.

1. installed : ensconced :: alleviated : _____

    Relationship: _____

    _____

2. clothes : purchased :: fish : _____

    Relationship: _____

    _____

3. indispensable : necessary :: extraneous : _____

    Relationship: _____

    _____

Name _____   Period _____

4. blood : clot :: gelatin : _____

Relationship: _____

_____

5. fiesta : party :: banquet : _____

Relationship: _____

_____

6. sketchy : character :: sunny : _____

Relationship: _____

_____

7. applauding : performance :: _____ : criminal

Relationship: _____

_____

8. compliment : flattery :: insult : _____

Relationship: _____

_____

9. stopped : impeded :: motivated : _____

Relationship: _____

_____

Name _____   Period _____

Frankenstein
Quiz: Prologue, Letters

Directions: *Choose the best answer for each of the following questions from the Prologue and Letters. Write the letter of the correct answer on the line provided.*

_____ 1. Who wrote the Prologue of *Frankenstein*?
   a. Mary Shelley
   b. Mary Wollstonecraft
   c. Percy Bysshe Shelley
   d. William Godwin

_____ 2. Which of the following works did *not* inspire *Frankenstein's* author?
   a. Shakespeare's *A Midsummer Night's Dream*
   b. Stoker's *Dracula*
   c. *Iliad*
   d. Milton's *Paradise Lost*

_____ 3. Which of the following is *not* a theme frequently addressed by Romantic writers?
   a. travel
   b. self-education
   c. adventure
   d. self-control

_____ 4. What is Walton attempting to locate?
   a. Northern passage through the Arctic
   b. South Pole
   c. Alaska
   d. an escaped fugitive

_____ 5. What does Walton desire when he writes the second letter?
   a. home-cooked food
   b. to see his sister
   c. a friend
   d. warmer clothing

_____ 6. What characteristic of Walton makes him an ideal listener of Frankenstein's story?
   a. Walton believes in the "marvelous."
   b. Walton is desperate to hear an interesting story.
   c. Walton is out-of-touch with reality.
   d. Walton is interested in science.

_____ 7. What odd sight do the sailors first see?
   a. dogs running wild
   b. a haggard man trying to board the ship
   c. a large man on a sledge
   d. Northern lights

_____ 8. Which of the following does *not* describe the man who boards Walton's ship?
   a. European
   b. healthy
   c. speaks English
   d. haggard

_____ 9. Why does the man agree to tell Walton his story?
   a. to entertain Walton
   b. to convince Walton to help him
   c. to receive advice
   d. to relieve himself of his guilt

_____ 10. What is Walton's role as the man tells his story?
   a. to take notes of the story
   b. to tape record the story
   c. to contact the police
   d. to only listen to the story

Vocabulary Quiz: Prologue and Letters

Directions: *Match the vocabulary words with the correct definition. Write the letter of the correct definition on the line provided.*

_____ 1. physiological

_____ 2. delineating

_____ 3. expedient

_____ 4. forebodings

_____ 5. satiate

_____ 6. enticement

_____ 7. endowments

_____ 8. solicitude

_____ 9. countenance

_____ 10. melancholy

a. look or expression of the face

b. strong inner feelings of a future misfortune or evil

c. concerned with the normal functioning of an organism

d. attributes of mind or body

e. means to an end; resource; method

f. something which leads one on with a desire or hope

g. to satisfy to the fullest

h. a gloomy state of mind

i. describing or outlining with precision

j. concern over someone or something

Frankenstein
Quiz: Chapters One–Two

Directions: *Answer the following questions from Chapters One–Two on a separate piece of paper using complete sentences. Give as many details as possible to support your answer.*

1. Explain how Victor Frankenstein's parents met.

2. Describe Victor's childhood.

3. Explain how Elizabeth comes into the Frankenstein home.

4. Describe Victor's relationship with Henry Clerval.

5. What authors and topics does Victor become obsessed with reading?

6. How does Victor learn about alchemy and natural science?

7. Describe Victor's first experience with lightning.

Vocabulary Quiz: Chapters One–Two

Directions: *Write the vocabulary word that best matches each definition, choosing from the word bank below. Write your answer on the line provided. Be careful to spell the word correctly as you write. Not all words will be used.*

indefatigable	recompensing	vehement	chimerical
interment	penury	solitude	tertiary
extort	reverential	ignoble	ineffectual

_____ 1. feeling or exhibiting deep respect

_____ 2. never tiring or yielding

_____ 3. of the third order, rank, stage, or formation

_____ 4. extreme poverty

_____ 5. of low character or quality

_____ 6. without satisfactory or satisfying effect

_____ 7. act or ceremony of burying

_____ 8. highly unrealistic

_____ 9. strongly or intensely emotional

_____ 10. to pay or give compensation for

Name _____ Period _____

Frankenstein
Quiz: Chapters Three—Five

Directions: *For each of the following statements, write "true" if the statement is true and "false" if the statement is false. For each of the false statements, use the lines below the statement to rewrite the sentence, making the statement true.*

_____ 1. Caroline Frankenstein hopes that Elizabeth and Victor marry each other.

_____

_____

_____ 2. Henry Clerval's father anxiously awaits his son's opportunity to attend

college. _____

_____

_____ 3. M. Krempe takes Victor under his wing and acts as his mentor. _____

_____

_____ 4. Victor studies human anatomy, how life is created, death, and decay.

_____

_____ 5. Technology as a positive, driving force appears repeatedly in the works of

the Romantic writers. _____

_____

_____ 6. Victor thinks his creation will be grateful to and appreciative of him.

_____

_____ 7. While forming his creature, Victor isolates himself from others so they will

not learn of his actions. _____

_____

_____ 8. After the creature comes to life, Victor watches it through a window.

_____

_____ 9. Victor is thrilled to see Henry Clerval in Ingolstadt. _____

_____

_____ 10. Henry asks Victor to write a letter to his mother and father. _____

_____

Name _____   Period _____

Vocabulary Quiz: Chapters Three—Five

Directions: *Choose the best vocabulary word for each of the following definitions. Write the letter of the correct answer on the line provided.*

_____ 1. forecasted or predicted
a. reprobated
b. odious
c. prognosticated
d. depravity

_____ 2. state of peace or calm
a. repose
b. dirge
c. dogmatism
d. supple

_____ 3. strong distaste, aversion, or objection
a. panegyric
b. precarious
c. profundity
d. repugnance

_____ 4. disapproved or condemned
a. irreparable
b. reprobated
c. chimerical
d. frantically

_____ 5. a brief review or summary
a. recapitulation
b. approbation
c. testimony
d. opprobrium

_____ 6. respectful or courteous regard
a. placid
b. congeal
c. glum
d. deference

_____ 7. arrogant assertions of one's opinions as truths
a. dogmatism
b. promontory
c. disdain
d. pandemonium

_____ 8. something that interferes or delays action or progress
a. ineffectual
b. hinderance
c. paroxysm
d. satiate

_____ 9. beginning to exist or appear
a. infamous
b. abyss
c. legacy
d. incipient

_____ 10. lack of energy or vitality
a. languor
b. mien
c. wantonly
d. immured

Frankenstein
Quiz: Chapters Six—Eight

Directions: *Answer the following questions from Chapters Six—Eight on a separate piece of paper using complete sentences. Give as many details as possible to support your answer.*

1. Tell how Justine comes to live with the Frankenstein family.

2. Describe William Frankenstein.

3. What do Victor and Clerval begin studying together?

4. Tell how William dies.

5. Explain why Victor feels that he has murdered his brother, William.

6. What evidence is used to charge Justine with William's murder?

7. Why does Victor not share who he believes murdered William?

8. How does Elizabeth attempt to defend Justine?

9. Why does Justine confess to William's murder?

Vocabulary Quiz: Chapters Six—Eight

Directions: *Match the vocabulary words with the correct definition. Write the letter of the correct definition on the line provided.*

_____ 1. odious

_____ 2. mien

_____ 3. irreparable

_____ 4. placid

_____ 5. dirge

_____ 6. delirium

_____ 7. depravity

_____ 8. candour

_____ 9. ignominious

_____ 10. approbation

a. incapable of being remedied

b. bearing or demeanor, as showing character or feelings

c. being open or sincere in speech or expression

d. state of violent excitement or emotions

e. approval; commendation

f. a funeral song to mourn the dead

g. state of being corrupt, wicked, or perverted

h. calm or undisturbed

i. hateful; detestable

j. discreditable; humiliating

Name _____ Period _____

Frankenstein
Quiz: Chapters Nine—Ten

Directions: *Choose the best answer for each of the following questions from Chapters Nine—Ten. Write the letter of the correct answer on the line provided.*

_____ 1. Victor responds to William and Justine's deaths by
   a. planning to hunt down the monster.
   b. becoming depressed and wanting to be alone.
   c. telling his family about the monster.
   d. taking his family and leaving Switzerland.

_____ 2. At night, Victor frequently
   a. searches for the monster.
   b. visits William's grave.
   c. studies the legalities of Justine's execution.
   d. rows his boat into the middle of the lake.

_____ 3. Why does Victor feel like he is the "true murderer" of William and Justine?
   a. He created William and Justine's murderer.
   b. By not speaking up about the monster, Victor caused Justine's execution.
   c. Both a and b
   d. None of the above

_____ 4. How does it seem the monster plans to seek revenge on Victor?
   a. follow Victor throughout the world
   b. not allow Victor to know of his whereabouts
   c. harm random people and frame Victor for murder
   d. harm Victor's family members

_____ 5. Which of the following best explains the Romantic writers' attitude toward nature?
   a. Nature was created for the pleasure of men.
   b. Nature can act as a soothing healing force.
   c. Nature was created as a source of products and materials.
   d. Nature should be worshipped as a living deity.

_____ 6. What ultimatum does the creature give Victor?
   a. locate a friend for the creature
   b. help the creature travel to a remote location
   c. change the creature's appearance to make him appear more human
   d. comply with the creature's demands or he will continue to murder people

_____ 7. Why does the creature say that he committed murder?
   a. Humans' abhorrence of him drove him to commit murder.
   b. Children had been especially cruel to the creature.
   c. The creature is unable to have children of his own
   d. The creature specifically hunted William because of his kinship to Victor.

_____ 8. Which choice best describes how the creature portrays himself when speaking to Victor?
   a. ill-educated and crude
   b. threatening and violent
   c. well-spoken and intelligent
   d. despondent and depressed

Name _____ Period _____

Vocabulary Quiz: Chapters Nine—Ten

Directions: *Write the vocabulary word that best matches each definition, choosing from the word bank below. Write your answer on the line provided. Be careful to spell the word correctly as you write. All words will be used only once.*

augmenting   epoch   diabolically
base   pallid   disdain
efface   precipitous
abyss   abhorred

_____ 1. extremely or impassably steep

_____ 2. morally low; dishonorable

_____ 3. look upon or treat with contempt

_____ 4. a particular period of time marked by distinctive features or events

_____ 5. enlarging in size, number, strength, or extent

_____ 6. wickedly; fiendishly

_____ 7. to wipe out or do away with

_____ 8. pale or faint in color

_____ 9. regarded with extreme aversion or loathing

_____ 10. deep chasm or cavity

Name _____ Period _____

Frankenstein
Quiz: Chapters Eleven—Twelve

Directions: *For each of the following statements, write "true" if the statement is true and "false" if the statement is false. For each of the false statements, use the lines below the statement to rewrite the sentence, making the statement true.*

_____ 1. After leaving Ingolstadt, the creature wanders in the forest and gradually learns how to use his senses. _____

_____

_____ 2. The creature first learns about fire when he sees a tree catch fire after being struck by lightning. _____

_____

_____ 3. The first humans the creature encounters offer him food and water.

_____

_____ 4. The creature observes a family consisting of an elderly blind man, his son, and daughter. _____

_____

_____ 5. The creature learns about family relationships, kindness, speech, and reading from watching the family. _____

_____

_____ 6. The DeLacey family has plenty of food and resources to supply their needs and wants. _____

_____

_____ 7. The creature helps the DeLacey family by cutting wood and placing it by their door each night. _____

_____

_____ 8. The creature thinks that if he can speak to humans, they will overlook his frightening appearance. _____

_____

_____ 9. The creature observes the DeLacey family for about four weeks. _____

_____

_____ 10. The creature views himself as superior to the DeLacey family and wonders what they would want him to teach them. _____

_____

_____

Name _____   Period _____

Vocabulary Quiz: Chapters Eleven—Twelve

Directions: *Choose the best vocabulary word for each of the following definitions. Write the letter of the correct answer on the line provided.*

_____ 1. dark; dull
a. transparent
b. opaque
c. filigreed
d. pensive

_____ 2. act of leaving one's country or region to settle in another
a. emigration
b. amplification
c. instigation
d. immigration

_____ 3. severe, rough, or harsh treatment
a. hysterical
b. depravity
c. inclemency
d. congeal

_____ 4. took dishonestly; stole
a. incubated
b. adduced
c. expired
d. purloined

_____ 5. dreamily or wistfully thoughtful
a. ludicrous
b. haggard
c. enigmatic
d. pensive

_____ 6. guessed; speculated
a. languished
b. immured
c. conjectured
d. lumbered

_____ 7. commanding respect because of age or dignity
a. venerable
b. imperious
c. finicky
d. immortal

_____ 8. perplexing; mysterious
a. antiquated
b. enigmatic
c. blemished
d. noisome

_____ 9. eagerly; zealously
a. illusory
b. wantonly
c. melancholy
d. ardently

_____ 10. persons who have the sole power of judging or determining
a. scions
b. throngs
c. arbiters
d. successors

Frankenstein
Quiz: Chapters Thirteen—Fourteen

Directions: Answer the following questions from Chapters Thirteen—Fourteen using complete sentences. Give as many details as possible to support your answer.

1. Whose arrival improves Felix's spirits?

2. How does this person's presence facilitate the creature's ability to speak and read?

3. How does the creature demonstrate his fear of encountering humans?

4. How does the creature view himself after hearing Volney's *Ruins of Empires*?

5. Describe the De Lacey family's background.

6. How does the Turk use Safie to ensure Felix's assistance?

7. Tell how Safie chafes against the cultural expectations of her.

8. Why is it ironic that Safie's father does not want her to marry Felix, a Christian?

Vocabulary Quiz: Chapters Thirteen—Fourteen

Directions: Match the vocabulary words with the correct definition. Write the letter of the correct definition on the line provided.

_____ 1. verdure

_____ 2. dissipates

_____ 3. cadence

_____ 4. scion

_____ 5. vagabond

_____ 6. tenets

_____ 7. immured

_____ 8. noisome

_____ 9. expostulate

_____ 10. Pittance

a. doctrines held by members of a group, profession, or movement

b. green vegetation

c. to reason earnestly with someone

d. person who wanders from place to place

e. small amount or share

f. secluded; confined

g. a descendant or offshoot

h. scatters in various directions

i. offensive; disgusting

j. rhythmic flow of sounds or words

Frankenstein
Quiz: Chapters Fifteen—Seventeen

Directions: *Choose the best answer for each of the following questions from Chapters Fifteen—Seventeen. Write the letter of the correct answer on the line provided.*

_____ 1. Which of the following is *not* a book which the creature reads after finding it in Victor's coat?
  a. Milton's *Paradise Lost*
  b. *Plutarch's Lives*
  c. Coleridge's *The Rime of the Ancient Mariner*
  d. Goethe's *The Sorrows of Werter*

_____ 2. After learning to read and gaining more knowledge,
  a. the creature decides to form a mate for himself.
  b. the creature decides to read all of the classic texts of the Western world.
  c. the creature tries to commit suicide.
  d. the creature realizes how much he is an outcast from society.

_____ 3. How does the creature plan to approach the DeLacey family?
  a. by bringing wood he has cut to their door.
  b. by approaching Felix and Agatha outside their home
  c. by talking to the father while the rest of the family is out of the home
  d. by taking food to the family

_____ 4. How does Felix react when he sees the creature?
  a. Felix beats the creature until he leaves the family's home.
  b. Felix thanks the creature for bringing wood to his family.
  c. Felix introduces the creature to Agatha and Safie.
  d. Felix asks the creature to eat dinner with the family.

_____ 5. How does the creature respond to the DeLacey family's departure?
  a. The creature cries and grieves his loss.
  b. The creature sets the DeLacey's cottage on fire.
  c. The creature removes sentimental items from the DeLacey's cottage.
  d. The creature follows the DeLacey family.

_____ 6. Why does the creature want to meet Victor?
  a. The creature wants to kill Victor.
  b. The creature wants Victor to tell him about his birth.
  c. The creature feels that Victor is the person most likely to offer him companionship.
  d. The creature wants to travel around the world with Victor.

_____ 7. What happens to the creature after he rescues a girl from drowning?
  a. He is shot.
  b. He is rewarded for his heroism.
  c. He is asked to have dinner with the girl's family.
  d. He disappears before anyone sees him.

_____ 8. What does the creature demand of Victor?
   a. The creature wants Victor to make a friend for him.
   b. The creature wants to be part of Victor's family.
   c. The creature wants Victor to make him a female companion.
   d. The creature wants Victor to change his appearance to make him more attractive.

_____ 9. How does the creature believe that he would benefit from Victor meeting his demand?
   a. The creature would be less angry if he wasn't lonely.
   b. The creature could meet a mate if he was more attractive.
   c. The creature would have someone to explore the world with.
   d. The creature would have a greater understanding of human nature.

_____ 10. How does the creature plan to stay abreast of Victor's progress?
   a. Victor is to write letters to the creature.
   b. The creature is going to live with Victor.
   c. Clerval is to act as an intermediary between Victor and the creature.
   d. The creature will watch Victor and reappear when Victor completes his task.

Vocabulary Quiz: Chapters Fifteen—Seventeen

Directions: *Write the vocabulary word that best matches each definition, choosing from the word bank below. Write your answer on the line provided. Be careful to spell the word correctly as you write. Words will be used only once.*

deprecate	wantonly	epithets
sagacity	vestige	malignity
instigate	succor	contemns
consternation		

_____ 1. maliciously or unjustifiably

_____ 2. to disapprove of

_____ 3. intense ill will; spite

_____ 4. to urge or provoke to some action or course

_____ 5. help, relief, or aid

_____ 6. treats or regards with disdain, scorn, or contempt

_____ 7. acuteness of mental faculty and soundness of

                 judgment

_____ 8. mark, trace, or evidence of something

_____ 9. words or phrases used as terms of abuse or

                 contempt

_____ 10. sudden alarming amazement, fear, or confusion

Frankenstein
Quiz: Chapters Eighteen—Twenty

Directions: *For each of the following statements, write "true" if the statement is true and "false" if the statement is false. For each of the false statements, use the lines below the statement to rewrite the sentence, making the statement true.*

_____ 1. Victor feels that he must travel around the world before he can marry Elizabeth. _____

_____

_____ 2. Victor thinks the monster will follow him to England and not harm the Frankenstein family in Switzerland. _____

_____

_____ 3. Victor does not want Henry Clerval to accompany him on the trip to England. _____

_____

_____ 4. Victor feels that the creature and his demand have created a barrier between himself and the rest of humanity. _____

_____

_____

_____ 5. Victor cannot bear to hear or think about anything associated with the monster he created. _____

_____

_____ 6. Victor sets up a lab in a cabin on the Falkland Islands. _____

_____

_____ 7. As the monster stands at the door, Victor destroys the female creature.

_____

_____

_____ 8. The monster threatens Victor by telling him, "I shall be with you on your wedding-night." _____

_____

_____ 9. Victor takes the remains of the female creature out to sea and throws them overboard. _____

_____

_____ 10. Victor attempts to sail his boat away from the Orkney Islands. _____

_____

Name _____ Period _____

Vocabulary Quiz: Chapters Eighteen—Twenty

Directions: *Choose the best vocabulary word for each of the following definitions. Write the letter of the correct answer on the line provided.*

_____ 1. directed or ordered to do something
   a. imprecated
   b. enjoined
   c. permeated
   d. averted

_____ 2. lack of self-restraint
   a. impotence
   b. disquieting
   c. chastise
   d. incommoded

_____ 3. great depth; seriousness
   a. aptitude
   b. antipathy
   c. indolence
   d. profundity

_____ 4. set free; liberated
   a. enfranchised
   b. endowed
   c. hastened
   d. ecstatic

_____ 5. exposed to or involving danger
   a. base
   b. scrupulous
   c. precarious
   d. ominous

_____ 6. prominently; to a great degree
   a. eminently
   b. wryly
   c. penury
   d. exuberantly

_____ 7. any cause of impairment, destruction, ruin, or frustration
   a. tertiary
   b. transgression
   c. blight
   d. chastise

_____ 8. diligent in application or attention
   a. glum
   b. melancholy
   c. sedulous
   d. sublime

_____ 9. not to be persuaded, moved, or affected by entreaties
   a. rueful
   b. inexorable
   c. assuaged
   d. ineffectual

_____ 10. marked with patches or spots of different colors
   a. tertiary
   b. impotence
   c. assuaged
   d. variegated

Frankenstein
Quiz: Chapters Twenty-One—Twenty-Three

Directions: *Answer the following questions from Chapters Twenty-One—Twenty-Three on a separate sheet of paper using complete sentences. Give as many details as possible to support your answer.*

1. Why do the townspeople think Victor is the murderer?

2. Who has been murdered?

3. How does Mr. Kirwin help Victor?

4. Why is Victor acquitted of the murder?

5. Why does Elizabeth think that Victor is depressed and troubled?

6. What does Victor think will occur between himself and the monster on his wedding-night?

7. How does Victor try to protect himself from the monster?

8. How does the monster fulfill his promise to be with Victor on his wedding-night?

9. How does the wedding-night tragedy adversely affect Alphonse Frankenstein?

10. How do the deaths change Victor's focus in life?

Vocabulary Quiz: Chapters Twenty-One—Twenty-Three

Directions: *Match the vocabulary words with the correct definition. Write the letter of the correct definition on the line provided.*

_____ 1. supposition

_____ 2. languid

_____ 3. visage

_____ 4. vexations

_____ 5. degradation

_____ 6. imperious

_____ 7. vanquished

_____ 8. enunciation

_____ 9. artifice

_____ 10. reverie

a. trickery; guile; deception

b. assumption; hypothesis

c. the face, usually with reference to shape, features, or expression

d. the act of clearly stating or declaring something

e. lowered in dignity, character, or rank

f. lacking in vigor or vitality

g. irritations; annoyances

h. conquered or subdued by superior force

i. intensely compelling

j. state of dreamy meditation or fanciful musing

Frankenstein
Quiz: Chapter 24—Continuation

Directions: *Choose the best answer for each of the following questions from Chapter Twenty-Four and the Continuation. Write the letter of the correct answer on the line provided.*

_____ 1. Where do Victor and the creature travel?
  a. They leave Geneva and head north through France and on to Scandinavia.
  b. They leave Geneva, cross the Mediterranean Sea, and venture south through Africa.
  c. They leave Geneva and head to the Mediterranean Sea where they board a ship bound for the Black Sea. They then journey north through Russia and to the Arctic Circle.
  d. They leave Geneva and head to the Mediterranean Sea where they board a ship bound for South America. They then journey through Brazil and Argentina to Antarctica.

_____ 2. How does the creature enable Victor to stay on his trail?
  a. At times, the creature stops and waits for Victor.
  b. The creature leaves hints and clues for Victor.
  c. The creature sends Victor a letter outlining his path.
  d. The creature makes sure that people in the area always see him.

_____ 3. How does the creature view humans while on his journey?
  a. The creature views humans as helpers. He freely utilizes their skills and assistance while on his journey.
  b. The creature views humans as resources. He takes what he needs from them while on his journey.
  c. The creature views humans as good Samaritans. He employs their help and assistance while on his journey.
  d. The creature views humans as enemies. He does not hesitate to frighten or steal from people while on his journey.

_____ 4. What natural event threatens Victor's safety?
  a. The ice breaks apart stranding Victor and his sled dogs on a floating piece of ice.
  b. An avalanche almost buries Victor and his sled dogs.
  c. The ice begins melting, threatening to send Victor and his sled dogs into the sea.
  d. A blizzard threatens the lives of Victor and his sled dogs.

_____ 5. Who does Victor feel guides him on his journey?
  a. Victor feels that he is guided by his own intuition.
  b. Victor feels that he is guided by the psychic link between himself and the creature.
  c. Victor feels that he is guided by the spirits of his dead friends and family.
  d. Victor feels that he is guided by nature spirits.

_____ 6. Which of the following best describes the situation aboard Walton's ship?
  a. The ship strikes an iceberg while attempting to navigate the ice floes.
  b. The ship is stuck between ice floes. The crew wants to turn around and head south.
  c. The ship runs out of fuel. The crew relaxes while waiting for more fuel to arrive.
  d. Disease has broken out on the ship. The crew sends for emergency medical care.

_____ 7. How has Walton spent most of his time since Victor has boarded his ship?
  a. tending to the sick crew members
  b. trying to prevent a mutiny on board the ship
  c. repairing the damaged ship
  d. listening to Victor's story

_____ 8. Who does Walton find with Victor?
a. Walton finds spirits with Victor's dead body.
b. Walton finds the monster with Victor's dead body.
c. Victor's body disappears from the ship.
d. Walton finds several crew members with Victor's dead body.

_____ 9. How does the monster feel now that Victor is dead?
a. The monster mourns Victor and regrets hurting him.
b. The monster is angry that Victor has died.
c. The monster feels vindicated that Victor has died.
d. The monster feels a new sense of freedom.

_____ 10. What does the creature do after Victor dies?
a. The creature asks to have Victor's body.
b. The creature becomes a crew member on Walton's ship.
c. The creature leaves the ship.
d. The creature commits suicide.

Vocabulary Quiz: Chapter Twenty-Four—Continuation

Directions: *Write the vocabulary word that best matches each definition, choosing from the word bank below. Write your answer on the line provided. Be careful to spell the word correctly as you write. Not all words will be used.*

abjuration	omnipotent	ignoble	contumely
repast	congeal	actuated	disencumbered
scoffing	dispositions	superfluous	procured

_____ 1. obtained by care, effort, or special means

_____ 2. the act of renouncing or recanting one's errors

_____ 3. contemptuous or humiliating treatment

_____ 4. mocking; jeering

_____ 5. to change from a soft or fluid state to a rigid or solid

state

_____ 6. a meal intended to be eaten

_____ 7. unnecessary or needless

_____ 8. freed from a burden

_____ 9. incited or moved to action

_____ 10. natural mental and emotional outlooks or moods

Name _____   Period _____

Frankenstein
Final Exam

Part A: Matching
Directions: Match the following characters with the correct description or action. Write the letter of the correct answer on the line provided.

_____ 1. Victor Frankenstein

_____ 2. Alphonse Frankenstein

_____ 3. William Frankenstein

_____ 4. Robert Walton

_____ 5. unnamed creature

_____ 6. Henry Clerval

_____ 7. Elizabeth Lavenza

_____ 8. Felix DeLacey

_____ 9. Mr. Kirwin

_____ 10. Justine Moritz

a. younger brother of Victor Frankenstein

b. beats creature until he leaves his home

c. wants a female companion

d. executed for William's death

e. creates a human-like monster

f. best friend of Victor Frankenstein

g. ship captain

h. defends Victor when he is accused of murder

i. family patriarch

j. strangled on her wedding-night

Part B: True/ False
Directions: For each of the following statements, decide whether it is true or false. If true, write "true" on the line provided; if false, write the word "false."

_____ 11. Caroline Frankenstein hopes that Elizabeth and Victor marry each other.

_____ 12. Technology as a positive, driving force appears repeatedly in the works of the Romantic writers.

_____ 13. Victor thinks his creation will be grateful to and appreciative of him.

_____ 14. After the creature comes to life, Victor watches it through a window.

_____ 15. The creature first learns about fire when he sees a tree catch fire after being struck by lightning.

_____ 16. The DeLacey family is quite well-to-do.

_____ 17. The creature thinks that if he can speak to humans, they will overlook his frightening appearance.

_____ 18. The creature helps the DeLacey family by cutting wood and placing it by their door each night.

_____ 19. Victor thinks the monster will follow him to England and not harm the Frankenstein family in Switzerland.

_____ 20. Victor sets up a lab in a cabin on the Falkland Islands.

_____ 21. The monster threatens Victor by telling him, "I shall be with you on your wedding-night."

_____ 22. Victor takes the remains of the female creature out to sea and throws them overboard.

Part C: Multiple Choice

Directions: Choose the letter of the best response. Write the letter of the correct answer on the line provided.

_____ 23. Which of the following is not a theme frequently addressed by Romantic writers?
a. travel
b. self-education
c. adventure
d. self-control

_____ 24. What is Walton attempting to locate?
a. Northern passage through the Arctic
b. South Pole
c. Alaska
d. an escaped fugitive

_____ 25. What is Walton's role as the man tells his story?
a. to take notes of the story
b. to tape record the story
c. to contact the police
d. to only listen to the story

_____ 26. Why does Victor feel like he is the "true murderer" of William and Justine?
a. He created William and Justine's murderer.
b. By not speaking up about the monster, Victor caused Justine's execution.
c. Both a and b
d. None of the above

_____ 27. Which of the following best explains the Romantic writers' attitude toward nature?
a. Nature was created for the pleasure of men.
b. Nature can act as a soothing, healing force.
c. Nature was created as a source of products and materials.
d. Nature should be worshipped as a living deity.

_____ 28. Which statement best describes how the creature portrays himself while speaking to Victor?
a. ill-educated and crude
b. threatening and violent
c. well-spoken and intelligent
d. despondent and depressed

_____ 29. How does the creature plan to approach the DeLacey family?
a. bring wood he has cut to their door
b. approach Felix and Agatha outside their home
c. talk to the father while the rest of the family is out of the home
d. take food to the family

_____ 30. How does Felix react when he sees the creature?
a. Felix beats the creature until he leaves the family's home.
b. Felix thanks the creature for bringing wood to his family.
c. Felix introduces the creature to Agatha and Safie.
d. Felix asks the creature to eat dinner with the family.

_____ 31. What does the creature demand of Victor?
a. The creature wants Victor to make a friend for him.
b. The creature wants to be part of Victor's family.
c. The creature wants Victor to make him a female companion.
d. The creature wants Victor to change his appearance to make him more attractive.

_____ 32. What natural event threatens Victor's safety?
a. The ice breaks apart stranding Victor and his sled dogs on a floating piece of ice.
b. An avalanche almost buries Victor and his sled dogs.
c. The ice begins melting, threatening to send Victor and his sled dogs into the sea.
d. A blizzard threatens the lives of Victor and his sled dogs.

_____ 33. What does the creature do after Victor dies?
a. The creature asks to have Victor's body.
b. The creature becomes a crew member on Walton's ship.
c. The creature leaves the ship.
d. The creature commits suicide.

Name _____   Period _____

Part D: Short Response (3-7 sentences each)

Directions: *Answer each of the following questions using complete sentences. Be sure to provide details to support your answer to EACH question. Use a sheet of lined paper for your answers and staple it to the back page of your test.*

34. Explain how Elizabeth comes into the Frankenstein home. _____

_____

_____

35. Why does Victor not share who he believes murdered William? _____

_____

_____

36. Describe the De Lacey family's background. _____

_____

_____

37. How do the deaths of Elizabeth and Alphonse change Victor's focus in life? _____

_____

_____

Part E: Vocabulary

Directions: *Match the following vocabulary words with the correct definition or synonym. Write the letter of the correct answer on the line provided.*

_____ 38. physiological

_____ 39. solicitude

_____ 40. indefatigable

_____ 41. ignoble

_____ 42. dogmatism

_____ 43. placid

_____ 44. disdain

_____ 45. venerable

_____ 46. immured

_____ 47. consternation

_____ 48. inexorable

_____ 49. languid

_____ 50. superfluous

a. calm or undisturbed

b. lacking in vigor or vitality

c. an attitude expressing excessive attentiveness

d. never tiring or yielding

e. secluded; confined

f. concerned with the normal functioning of an organism

g. of low character of quality

h. not to be persuaded, moved, or affected by entreaties

i. commanding respect because of age or dignity

j. unnecessary or needless; extra

k. arrogant assertions of one's opinions as truths

l. sudden alarming amazement, fear, or confusion

m. look upon or treat with contempt

Name _____   Period _____

Frankenstein
Final Exam: Multiple Choice

Directions: *Circle the letter of the best response to each question. OR, if you have a separate answer sheet, fill in the bubble of the correct response on your answer document.*

Part A: Characters
Choose the letter of the BEST character for each description.

1. Younger brother of Victor Frankenstein
   a. Alphonse Frankenstein
   b. Henry Frankenstein
   c. Felix Frankenstein
   d. William Frankenstein
2. Beats creature until he leaves his home
   a. Felix DeLacey
   b. Victor Frankenstein
   c. father DeLacey
   d. Henry Clerval
3. Wants a female companion
   a. Robert Walton
   b. unnamed creature
   c. Victor Frankenstein
   d. William Frankenstein
4. Executed for William's death
   a. Mr. Kirwin
   b. M. Krempe
   c. Justine Moritz
   d. Henry Clerval
5. Creates a human-like monster
   a. Felix DeLacey
   b. Victor Frankenstein
   c. Justine Moritz
   d. Robert Walton
6. Best friend of Victor Frankenstein
   a. Caroline Beaufort
   b. Mr. Kirwin
   c. Elizabeth Lavenza
   d. Henry Clerval
7. Ship captain
   a. Alphonse Frankenstein
   b. Robert Walton
   c. M. Krempe
   d. William Frankenstein
8. Defends Victor when he is accused of murder
   a. unnamed creature
   b. Alphonse Frankenstein
   c. Mr. Kirwin
   d. M. Krempe
9. Family patriarch
   a. Henry Clerval
   b. Victor Frankenstein
   c. William Frankenstein
   d. Alphonse Frankenstein
10. Strangled on her wedding-night
    a. Elizabeth Lavenza
    b. Caroline Beaufort
    c. Justine Moritz
    d. Agatha DeLacey

Part B: Plot
Choose the letter of the best response to each question.

11. Which of the following is *not* a theme frequently addressed by Romantic writers?
    a. travel
    b. self-education
    c. adventure
    d. self-control
12. What is Walton attempting to locate?
    a. Northern passage through the Arctic
    b. South Pole
    c. Alaska
    d. an escaped fugitive
13. What is Walton's role as the man tells his story?
    a. to take notes of the story
    b. to tape record the story
    c. to contact the police
    d. to only listen to the story

14. What expectation does Caroline Frankenstein have of Elizabeth and Victor?
    a. They will be best friends.
    b. They will marry each other.
    c. They will act like siblings.
    d. They will be brother and sister-in-law.

15. How do the Romantic writers frequently portray technology?
    a. positive, driving force
    b. necessary for human advancement
    c. a positive or negative force depending on how it is used
    d. the eventual downfall of humanity

16. How does Victor think his creation will feel toward him?
    a. grateful and appreciative
    b. angry and resentful
    c. loving and kind
    d. cool and unattached

17. What does Victor do after the creature comes to life?
    a. watch it through a window
    b. flee from his lab
    c. teach the creature about his body
    d. provide food and clothes for the creature

18. Why does Victor feel like he is the "true murderer" of William and Justine?
    a. He created William and Justine's murderer.
    b. By not speaking up about the monster, Victor caused Justine's execution.
    c. Both a and b
    d. None of the above

19. Which of the following best explains the Romantic writers' attitude toward nature?
    a. Nature was created for the pleasure of man.
    b. Nature can act as a soothing, healing force.
    c. Nature was created as a source of products and materials.
    d. Nature should be worshipped as a living deity.

20. Which statement best describes how the creature portrays himself while speaking to Victor?
    a. ill-educated and crude
    b. threatening and violent
    c. well-spoken and intelligent
    d. despondent and depressed

21. Which best describes the creature's first experience with fire?
    a. He sees lightning catch a tree on fire.
    b. He burns his hand when he places it in a fire.
    c. He uses a fire to cook meat.
    d. He burns down the DeLacey's cottage.

22. Which best describes the DeLacey family's current situation?
    a. wealthy and well-connected
    b. poor and struggling to survive
    c. anarchists who attempt to overthrow the government
    d. hiding from the Turk

23. What skill does the creature feel that he needs to have before he can approach humans?
    a. the ability to read
    b. the ability to hunt
    c. the ability to speak
    d. the ability to cook

24. How does the creature help the DeLacey family?
    a. tends the family's garden
    b. places firewood by the family's door
    c. protects the family from robbers
    d. teaches Safie to speak French

25. How does the creature plan to approach the DeLacey family?
    a. bring wood he has cut to their door
    b. approach Felix and Agatha outside their home
    c. talk to the father while the rest of the family is out of the home
    d. take food to the family

26. How does Felix react when he sees the creature?
    a. Felix beats the creature until he leaves the family's home.
    b. Felix thanks the creature for bringing wood to his family.
    c. Felix introduces the creature to Agatha and Safie.
    d. Felix asks the creature to eat dinner with the family.

27. What does the creature demand of Victor?
    a. The creature wants Victor to make him a friend.
    b. The creature wants to be part of Victor's family.
    c. The creature wants Victor to make him a female companion.
    d. The creature wants Victor to make him more attractive.

28. Where does Victor set up his lab?
    a. Falkland Islands
    b. Orkney Islands
    c. Canary Islands
    d. Galapagos Islands

29. What threat does the creature communicate to Victor?
    a. "I will pursue you to the ends of the earth."
    b. "I will murder your family."
    c. "I will make your life miserable."
    d. "I will be with you on your wedding-night."

30. What does Victor do with the remains of the female creature?
    a. burns them
    b. gives them to the male creature
    c. throws them overboard
    d. tosses them into the woods

31. What natural event threatens Victor's safety?
    a. The ice breaks apart, stranding Victor and his sled dogs on a floating piece of ice.
    b. An avalanche almost buries Victor and his sled dogs.
    c. The ice begins melting threatening to send Victor and his sled dogs into the sea.
    d. A blizzard threatens the lives of Victor and his sled dogs.

32. What does the creature do after Victor dies?
    a. The creature asks to have Victor's body.
    b. The creature becomes a crew member on Walton's ship.
    c. The creature leaves the ship.
    d. The creature commits suicide.

Part C: Vocabulary
Circle the letter of the best vocabulary word for each definition or synonym, OR fill in the bubble of the correct response on your answer sheet.

33. Concerned with the normal functioning of an organism
    a. expedient
    b. psychological
    c. melancholy
    d. physiological

34. An attitude expressing excessive attentiveness
    a. solicitude
    b. soliloquy
    c. chimerical
    d. penury

35. Never tiring or yielding
    a. satiate
    b. ineffectual
    c. countenance
    d. indefatigable

36. Of low character or quality
    a. vehement
    b. ignoble
    c. languor
    d. irreparable

37. Arrogant assertions of one's opinions as truths
    a. dogmatism
    b. repose
    c. deference
    d. lassitude

38. Calm or undisturbed
    a. promontory   c. placid
    b. delirium   d. mien

39. Look upon or treat with contempt
    a. epoch   c. augmenting
    b. abyss   d. disdain

40. Commanding respect because of age or dignity
    a. enigmatic   c. scion
    b. venerable   d. vestige

41. Secluded; confined
    a. immured   c. ardently
    b. noisome   d. deprecate

42. Sudden alarming amazement, fear, or confusion
    a. dirge   c. consternation
    b. execration   d. blight

43. Not to be persuaded, moved, or affected by entreaties
    a. feint   c. insuperable
    b. inexorable   d. enticement

44. Unnecessary or needless; extra
    a. omnipotent   c. politic
    b. sanguinary   d. superfluous

45. Obtained by care or special means
    a. congeal   c. procured
    b. actuated   d. modulated

46. Irritations; annoyances
    a. vales   c. vexations
    b. abjuration   d. paroxysms

47. Any cause of impairment, destruction, ruin, or frustration
    a. superscription   c. blight
    b. benignity   d. haggard

48. Conquered or subdued by superior force
    a. vanquished   c. actuated
    b. modulated   d. disencumbered

49. Doctrines held by members of a group, profession, or movement
    a. tenets   c. pittances
    b. arbiters   d. disquisitions

50. Dreamily or wistfully thoughtful
    a. self-deceit   c. ignoble
    b. noisome   d. pensive

Frankenstein
Teacher Guide
Sample Agenda

Below is a sample unit plan integrating all aspects of this *Frankenstein Literature Guide* for a 45-50 minute class.

Week One

Day One: Begin introducing themes and elements of the novel through *Pre-Reading Ideas and Activities* (p. 6). You may want to have students explore the modern equivalent of the novel's themes by assigning the *Pre-Reading Activity: Biological Scientific Research* (p. 7). Assign due dates for extended pre-reading activities. Introduce the *Author Biography* activity (pp. 10-11).

Day Two: Complete *Standards Focus: Genre, Romanticism: Gothic/ Science Fiction Novel* activity (pp. 12-13). Introduce *Standards Focus: Genre, Mythology: Frankenstein, or the Modern Prometheus* (pp. 14-15); finish for homework if necessary.

Day Three: Explore the *Allusions, Terminology, and Expressions* (pp. 16-20), as well as the *Vocabulary List* (p. 21) for reference. You can either have students find their own definitions in a dictionary or read the definitions to them, using pages 130-131 for reference. You may also want to allocate time for students to work on other *Pre-Reading Activities*. Introduce/ explain the *Note-Taking and Summarizing Activity* on page 22. Begin reading the Prologue and Letters; begin *Note-Taking and Summarizing* (p. 23) and *Comprehension Check* questions (p. 24) for the Prologue and Letters. Depending upon your students, you may want to have them do some reading at home to be sure to finish the chapters tomorrow.

Day Four: Finish reading the Prologue and Letters; finish *Note-Taking and Summarizing* (p. 23) and *Comprehension Check* questions (p. 24) for the Prologue and Letters.

Day Five: Have students complete and discuss *Standards Focus: Mood and Tone* (pp. 25-27). Complete *Assessment Preparation: Vocabulary in Context* (pp. 28-29) for homework. Be sure to go over or do one or two examples in class before sending home to work independently.

Week Two

Day One: Administer *Quiz: Prologue, Letters* (p. 97) and *Vocabulary Quiz: Prologue, Letters* (p. 98). Begin reading Chapters 1-2; begin *Note-Taking and Summarizing* (p. 30) and *Comprehension Check* questions (p. 31). Depending upon your students, you may want to have them do some reading at home to be sure to finish the chapters tomorrow.

Day Two: Finish reading Chapters 1-2; finish *Note-Taking and Summarizing* (p. 30) and *Comprehension Check* questions (p. 31).

Day Three: Complete and discuss *Standards Focus: Character Interactions* (pp. 32-33). Have students complete *Assessment Preparation: Spelling, Punctuation, and Capitalization* (pp. 34-35) for homework. Be sure to go over or do one or two examples in class before sending home to work independently.

Day Four: Administer *Quiz: Chapters 1-2* (p. 99) and included *Vocabulary Quiz*. Begin reading Chapters 3-5 and begin *Note-Taking and Summarizing* (p. 37) and *Comprehension Check* questions (p. 38). Depending upon your students, you may want to have them do some reading at home to be sure to finish the chapters tomorrow.

Day Five: Finish Chapters 3-5 and *Note-Taking* (p. 37) and *Comprehension Check* questions (p. 38).

Week Three

Day One: Have students complete and discuss *Standards Focus: Literary Archetypes* (pp. 39-41); Have students complete *Assessment Preparation: Vocabulary in Context* (pp.42-43) for homework. Be sure to go over or do one or two examples in class before sending home to work independently.

Day Two: Administer *Quiz: Chapters 3-5* (p. 100) and *Vocabulary Quiz: Chapters 3-5* (p. 101).

Day Three: Begin reading Chapters 6-8, beginning *Note-Taking* (p. 44) *Comprehension Check* questions (p. 45) for Chapters 6-8. Depending upon your students, you may want to have them do some reading at home to be sure to finish the chapters tomorrow.

Day Four: Finish reading Chapters 6-8, *Note-Taking* (p. 44) and *Comprehension Check* questions (p. 45).

Day Five: Have students complete and discuss *Standards Focus: Imagery* (pp. 46-47); complete *Assessment Preparation: Verb Tense* (pp. 48-49) for homework. Be sure to go over or do one or two examples in class before sending home to work independently.

Week Four

Day One: Administer *Quiz: Chapters 6-8* (p. 102) and included *Vocabulary Quiz.*

Day Two: Begin reading Chapters 9-10, begin *Note-Taking* (p. 50) and *Comprehension Check* questions (p. 51). Depending upon your students, you may want to have them do some reading at home to be sure to finish the chapters tomorrow.

Day Three: Finish reading Chapters 9-10, finish *Note-Taking* (p. 50) and *Comprehension Check* questions (p. 51).

Day Four: Have students complete and discuss *Standards Focus: Foreshadowing* (pp. 53-55); Have students complete *Assessment Preparation: Precise Vocabulary* (pp. 56-58) for homework. Be sure to go over or do one or two examples in class before sending home to work independently.

Day Five: Administer *Quiz: Chapters 9-10* (p. 103) and *Vocabulary Quiz: Chapters 9-10* (p. 104). Begin reading Chapters 11-12 and complete *Note-Taking* (p. 59) and *Comprehension Check* questions (p. 60). Depending upon your students, you may want to have them do some reading at home to be sure to finish the chapters next class.

Week Five

Day One: Finish reading Chapters 11-12, *Note-Taking* (p. 59) and *Comprehension Check* questions (p. 60).

Day Two: Have students complete and discuss *Standards Focus: Symbolism* (pp. 61-62). Have students complete *Assessment Preparation: Complements* (pp. 63-64) for homework. Be sure to go over or do one or two examples in class before sending home to work independently.

Day Three: Administer *Quiz: Chapters 11-12* (p. 105) and *Vocabulary Quiz: Chapters 11-12* (p. 106). Begin reading Chapters 13-14 and complete *Note-Taking* (p. 65) and *Comprehension Check* questions (p. 66). Depending upon your students, you may want to have them do some reading at home to be sure to finish the chapters tomorrow.

Day Four: Finish reading Chapters 13-14, finish *Note-Taking* (p. 65) and *Comprehension Check* questions (p. 66).

Day Five: Have students complete and discuss *Standards Focus: Political and Philosophical Approach* (pp. 67-69); Have students complete *Assessment Preparation: Etymology* (pp. 70-72) for homework. Be sure to go over or do one or two examples in class before sending home to work independently.

Week Six

Day Two: Administer *Quiz: Chapters 13-14* (p. 107) and included *Vocabulary Quiz.* Begin reading Chapters 15-17, beginning *Note-Taking* (p. 73) and *Comprehension Check* questions (p. 74). Depending upon your students, you may want to have them do some reading at home to be sure to finish the chapters tomorrow.

Day Three: Finish reading Chapters 15-17, finishing *Note-Taking* (p. 73) and *Comprehension Check* questions (p. 74).

Day Four: Have students complete and discuss *Standards Focus: Point of View* (pp. 75-76); Have students complete *Assessment Preparation: Clauses* (pp. 77-78) for homework. Be sure to go over or do one or two examples in class before sending home to work independently.

Day Five: Administer *Quiz: Chapters 15-17* (p. 108) and *Vocabulary Quiz: Chapters 15-17* (p. 109). Begin reading Chapters 18-20, beginning *Note-Taking* (p. 79) and *Comprehension Check* questions (p. 80). Depending upon your students, you may want to have them do some reading at home to be sure to finish the chapters tomorrow.

Week Seven

Day One: Finish reading Chapters 18-20, finishing *Note-Taking* (p. 79) and *Comprehension Check* questions (p. 80).

Day Two: Have students complete and discuss *Standards Focus: Characterization* (pp. 81-82). Have students complete *Assessment Preparation: Base Words/ Root Words/ Affixes* (pp. 83-84) for homework. Be sure to go over or do one or two examples in class before sending home to work independently.

Day Three: Administer *Quiz: Chapters 18-20* (p. 110) and *Vocabulary Quiz: Chapters 18-20* (p. 111). Begin reading Chapters 21-23, beginning *Note-Taking* (p. 85) and *Comprehension Check* questions (p. 86). Depending upon your students, you may want to have them do some reading at home to be sure to finish the chapters tomorrow.

Day Four: Finish reading Chapters 21-23, finish *Note-Taking* (p. 85) and *Comprehension Check* questions (p. 86).

Day Five: Have students complete and discuss *Standards Focus: Historical Themes and Issues* (pp. 87-88); Have students complete *Assessment Preparation: Sentence Structure* (pp. 89-90) for homework. Be sure to go over or do one or two examples in class before sending home to work independently.

Week Eight

Day One: Administer *Quiz: Chapters 21-23* (p. 112) and included *Vocabulary Quiz*. Begin reading Chapter 24–Continuation, beginning *Note-Taking* (p. 91) and *Comprehension Check* questions (p. 92). Depending upon your students, you may want to have them do some reading at home to be sure to finish the chapters tomorrow.

Day Two: Finish reading Chapters 24—Continuation; finish *Note-Taking* (p. 91) and *Comprehension Check* questions (p. 92).

Day Three: Have students complete and discuss *Standards Focus: Themes* (pp. 93-94). Have students complete *Assessment Preparation: Analogies* (pp. 95-96) for homework. Be sure to go over or do one or two examples in class before sending home to work independently.

Day Four: Administer *Quiz: Chapter 24—Continuation* (p. 113) and *Vocabulary Quiz: Chapter 24 and Continuation* (p. 114).

Day Five: Review the novel by revisiting students' *Note-Taking Guides* and discussing the *Comprehension Check Questions*. Assign or let students select a *Post-Reading Activity* (p. 132) or a writing assignment from *Essay/ Writing Ideas* (p. 133), or both.

Week Nine

Day One: Give either version of the *Final Exam* (pp. 115-118 or pp. 119-122) or some form of *Alternative Assessment* (p. 132). Have students write an essay from the *Essay/ Writing Ideas* (pp. 133-134). You may want to set aside an additional class period for students to share their completed Post-Reading Activities or Alternative Assessments.

Notes for the Teacher

Not all activities and worksheets in this guide must be used. They are here to help you, so that you have some options to use with your students. **Please do not feel pressure to use everything!** We have worked hard to create a variety of helpful materials for you to choose from. Pick and choose materials that fit the needs of *your* students in *your* classroom, in *your* timeframe! Here are a few notes about his guide:

1. Page numbers referred to in this Literature Guide are from the Barnes & Noble Classics Edition, ISBN 978-1-59308-005-1, ©2003.
2. Journal Topics (pages 8-9) can be used while reading or after reading each chapter, as extra writing opportunities. These prompts also work well as end-of-unit assessment.
3. Both the *Note-Taking and Summarizing* activities and *Comprehension Check* questions are there to help your students get the most out of the novel. Depending upon your students and their needs, you may want to have them do one or the other, alternate, or do both.
4. The vocabulary in this novel can be difficult. We put together a list of words that we felt students should know for state and national assessments, SAT Exams, etc., or that we felt they would actually use or see again within a reasonable period of time. It is our conclusion that the unfamiliar words in *Frankenstein* are far too numerous and/or difficult for students at the regular grade level for the purposes of this guide. You may want to offer extra credit to students for defining words they find particularly interesting or difficult, or for the well-advanced student, you may wish to make this a requirement. An extended vocabulary list is below:

panegyric (45)	incommoded (106)	insuperable (168)
consummation (50)	execration (114)	sanguinary (170)
lassitude (55)	disquisitions (128)	politic (172)
discompose (60)	imprecate (139)	torpor (181)
antipathy (65)	benignity (142)	truce (182)
encomiums (66)	feint (146)	omnipotent (189)
dilatoriness (68)	undulations (147)	expire (193)
salubrious (68)	haggard (148)	acme (195)
unremitted (71)	treble (150)	vales (196)
promontory (74)	variegated (154)	invective (197)
adduced (81)	contrary (156)	avail (198)
timorous (82)	alleging (158)	asseverations (207)
perdition (85)	sublime (159)	auguries (210)
avowal (87)	superscription (161)	modulated (212)
supple (98)	tremulous (163)	opprobrium (218)

5. For many of the vocabulary activities, a good dictionary with etymology is needed. Students should have access to a good dictionary in the classroom as well as at home. Students can also refer to a site such as *Dictionary.com* to complete their work.
6. *Post-Reading Activities and Alternative Assessment* ideas are located on page 132. These project ideas can be used in addition to a written test or in place of it. Project rubrics are located on pages 135-136. Please note that the rubrics are slightly different: *Project Rubric A* is recommended for projects that have a small written element that does NOT have to be researched. *Project Rubric B* is recommended for projects that include a research component in which sources must be cited.
7. *Essay/Writing Ideas* are located on pages 133-134. Often, having students choose ONE topic from 2-3 essay topics that you have chosen ahead of time, in addition to their written test, works well. Many of these options, as well as the Journal Topics on pages 8-9, can also work as a process essay during your teaching of *Frankenstein*.
8. In reference to the activity on page 28: Due to the difficult nature of the vocabulary words, you may wish to have students write the dictionary definition first, then paraphrase it, or write it in their own words.

Frankenstein
Summary of the Novel by Chapter

Prologue

Mary Shelley's Prologue, assumed to be written by her husband in Mary's voice, states that the novel resulted from a writing contest between Mary Shelley, Percy Bysshe Shelley, and Lord Byron. While spending the summer in Switzerland, the three authors decided to see who could write the best ghost story.

Letters

While trying to sail to the North Pole, English explorer Robert Walton writes a series of letters to his sister, Margaret Saville. In Letters Two and Three, Walton comments on how lonely he is and how he is looking forward to the challenge of his voyage. In Letter Four, Walton shares that while his ship is stuck between two sheets of ice, the crew sees a man on a sledge about half a mile from the ship. The next day, a haggard second man on a sledge boards the ship and agrees to tell Walton his story.

Chapter One

The stranger on the ship, Victor Frankenstein, begins telling his life story. Victor is born into a well-to-do Swiss family. When Victor is a child, the Frankenstein family adopts Elizabeth Lavenza and decides that Elizabeth and Victor should someday marry.

Chapter Two

Victor and Elizabeth become best friends as they grow older and enjoy many happy times with their close friend, Henry Clerval. Victor becomes intrigued with natural science, occult science, alchemy, and electricity.

Chapter Three

Victor leaves Geneva, Switzerland, to attend the university at Ingolstadt. At the university, Victor decides to pursue a career in the sciences.

Chapter Four

Victor isolates himself while studying the creation of life, human anatomy, and the process of death and decay. With the intent of creating physically and morally-superior beings, Victor decides to create a living creature.

Chapter Five

During a storm, Victor brings his creature to life, but is horrified by what he has created. In Ingolstadt, Victor sees Henry Clerval who has also come to the university. After spending so much time working in isolation, Victor falls ill. Henry nurses his friend back to health, but knows nothing about Victor's creation since the monster has disappeared.

Chapter Six

Victor recovers as Henry begins his studies in Ingolstadt. Victor learns that Justine Moritz, a family friend, is now living with the Frankenstein family in Geneva.

Chapter Seven

Victor receives a letter from his father stating that Victor's youngest brother, William, has been killed. When he arrives in Geneva, Victor sees his monstrous creation near the spot where William was murdered. Justine Moritz is arrested for William's murder, and Victor does not share with the police his belief that his creation, whom he has told no one about, actually murdered William.

Chapter Eight

Even though Justine is truly innocent, she is executed for William's murder. Victor keeps his creation a secret, but feels immense guilt that his creation is responsible for the deaths of two people.

Chapter Nine

Victor and his family visit their home at Belrive. While there, Victor visits Chamounix alone.

Chapter Ten

Victor hikes to the summit of Montanvert and spots his creation moving quickly and agilely through the ice field. The monster convinces Victor to listen to his story.

Chapter Eleven

The monster tells Victor of his distress at being mocked and derided by humans. One night the creature finds shelter in a hovel from which he can observe an elderly man, De Lacey, and his two children, Agatha and Felix.

Chapter Twelve

From observing the family for several months, the monster learns to speak some basic words. He becomes increasingly attached to the family and surreptitiously gathers firewood to leave by their door each night.

Chapter Thirteen

A beautiful woman, Safie, arrives at the cottage. The creature learns world history by observing the family when Felix instructs Safie.

Chapter Fourteen

De Lacey lost his wealth and social status by trying to help a falsely-accused Turk escape from a French prison. While the Turk has deserted his benefactors, his daughter, Safie, and Felix have fallen in love with each other.

Chapter Fifteen

After the creature teaches himself to read, he peruses several classic works, as well as Victor's notes on his formation. The creature desires human companionship and presents himself to the family he has been observing. Felix sends the monster away, crushing the being's faith in humankind.

Chapter Sixteen

Devastated by rejection, the monster decides to seek revenge on his creator. Near Geneva, the being meets young William Frankenstein. When the monster learns of William's connection to Victor, the creature strangles and kills the boy.

Chapter Seventeen

The monster demands that Victor create a mate for him, and states that he will no longer kill once he enjoys some companionship. Skeptically and begrudgingly, Victor agrees to form a female mate for his invention.

Chapter Eighteen

Victor experiences doubts about creating another being, but decides to travel to England where he will prepare to create another monster.

Chapter Nineteen

Henry Clerval and Victor travel through England and Scotland. When Henry stays in England, Victor continues on to the remote Orkney Islands where he sets up a lab in which to build his creation.

Chapter Twenty

Victor decides that creating another monster poses too great a risk and destroys his work. The creature sees Victor doing so and promises that he will be with Victor on his wedding-night. Victor rows a boat into the middle of a lake where he dumps his work and instruments. When he arrives on the shore, Victor is arrested for murder.

Chapter Twenty–One

Victor learns that Henry Clerval has been found murdered and recognizes the tell-tale signs of strangulation by the monster. After being sick for two months, Victor is released from jail because of a lack of evidence.

Chapter Twenty–Two

Victor returns to Geneva and marries Elizabeth. He feels that the monster will try to attack him on his wedding-night.

Chapter Twenty–Three

While enjoying a walk on their wedding-night, Victor sends Elizabeth inside so he can prepare for his encounter with the monster. The monster then attacks and kills Elizabeth. A few days later, Victor's father dies from grief. Victor decides to dedicate his life to locating and destroying the monster.

Chapter Twenty–Four

Victor leaves Geneva and tracks the monster to the Arctic where he meets Walton. Victor asks Walton to continue searching for the monster after Victor dies.

Continuation

Walton writes a letter to his sister stating that he believes Victor's story. When Victor dies on the ship, the monster appears and weeps over his maker's body. Saying he regrets his evil nature, the monster says that he wants to die, too, and departs from the ship.

Frankenstein
Vocabulary List with Definitions

Prologue, Letters
1. physiological (9) - concerned with the normal functioning of an organism
2. delineating (9) - describing or outlining with precision or detail
3. expedient (9) – resource; method; a means to an end
4. forebodings (10) – bad omens; strong inner feelings of a future misfortune or evil
5. satiate (11) – satisfy; to gratify to the fullest
6. enticement (13) – temptation; something that leads one forward with desire or hope
7. endowments (15) – characteristics; attributes of mind or body
8. solicitude (19) – attention; concern for someone or something
9. countenance (21) – face; look or expression of the face
10. melancholy (25) – sad; a gloomy state of mind

Chapters One–Two
1. indefatigable (27) – unending; never tiring or yielding
2. interment (28) – burial; act or ceremony of burying
3. recompensing (29) – reimbursing; to pay or give compensation for
4. penury (30) – extreme poverty
5. reverential (31) – respectful; feeling or exhibiting deep respect
6. vehement (34) – intense; strongly or extremely emotional
7. ignoble (35) – base; of low character or quality
8. chimerical (36) – imaginary; highly unrealistic
9. tertiary (37) – third; of the third order, rank, stage, or formation
10. ineffectual (39) – unsatisfying; without satisfaction

Chapters Three–Five
1. prognosticated (40) – predicted; forecasted future events
2. repose (41) – peace; state of restfulness or calm
3. repugnance (42) – repulsion; strong distaste, aversion, or objection
4. reprobated (43) – disapproved of or condemned

5. recapitulation (44) – restatement; a brief review or summary
6. deference (46) – admiration; respectful or courteous regard
7. dogmatism (48) – stubbornness; arrogant assertions of one's opinions as truths
8. hinderance (sp. hindrance) (52) – obstacle; something that interferes or delays action or progress
9. incipient (54) – new; budding; beginning to exist or appear
10. languor (56) – lethargy; lack of energy or vitality

Chapters Six–Eight
1. odious (62) – hateful; detestable
2. mien (64) – appearance; bearing or demeanor, as showing character or feelings
3. irreparable (72) – permanent; incapable of being fixed or remedied
4. placid (73) – peaceful; calm or undisturbed
5. dirge (74) – a funeral song which mourns the dead
6. delirium (76) – frenzy; a state of violent excitement or uncontrollable emotion
7. depravity (78) – corruption; state of being corrupt, wicked, or perverted
8. candour (sp. candor) (79) – frankness; being open or sincere in speech or expression
9. ignominious (80) – shameful; deserving of humiliation or shame
10. approbation (83) - approval; an official commendation or authorization

Chapters Nine–Ten
1. augmenting (88) – enlarging in size, number, strength, or extent
2. base (89) – morally low; dishonorable
3. efface (90) – to wipe out or do away with
4. abyss (91) – deep chasm or cavity
5. epoch (92) – a particular period of time marked by distinctive features or events
6. pallid (93) – pale or faint in color
7. precipitous (95) – extremely or impassably steep
8. abhorred (96) – regarded with extreme aversion or loathing
9. diabolically (97) – wickedly; fiendishly
10. disdain (98) – look upon or treat with contempt

Chapters Eleven–Twelve
1. opaque (101) – dense; solid
2. emigration (103) – act of leaving one's country or region to settle in another
3. inclemency (105) – harsh unpleasantness
4. purloined (105) – took dishonestly; stole
5. pensive (107) – dreamily or wistfully thoughtful
6. conjectured (108) – guessed; speculated
7. venerable (109) – commanding respect because of age or dignity
8. enigmatic (110) – perplexing; mysterious
9. ardently (111) – eagerly; zealously
10. arbiters (113) – persons who have the sole power of judging or determining

Chapters Thirteen–Fourteen
1. verdure (115) – green vegetation
2. dissipates (116) – scatters in various directions
3. cadence (117) – rhythmic flow of sounds or words
4. scion (118) – a descendant or offshoot
5. vagabond (119) – person who wanders from place to place
6. tenets (123) – doctrines held by members of a group, profession, or movement
7. immured (123) – secluded; confined
8. noisome (124) – offensive; disgusting
9. expostulate (125) – to reason earnestly
10. pittance (125) – small amount or share

Chapters Fifteen–Seventeen
1. deprecate (127) – to disapprove of
2. sagacity (130) – acuteness of mental faculty and soundness of judgment
3. instigate (134) – to urge or provoke to some action or course
4. consternation (134) – sudden alarming amazement, fear, or confusion
5. wantonly (135) – maliciously or unjustifiably
6. vestige (137) – mark, trace, or evidence of something
7. succor (sp. *succour*) (138) – help, relief, or aid
8. epithets (141) – words or phrases used as terms of abuse or contempt
9. malignity (142) – intense ill will; spite
10. contemns (144) – treats or regards with disdain, scorn, or contempt

Chapters Eighteen–Twenty
1. enjoined (149) – directed or ordered to do something
2. enfranchised (152) – set free; liberated
3. sedulous (153) – diligent in application or attention; painstaking
4. variegated (154) – marked with patches or spots of different colors; multicolored
5. eminently (155) – extremely; to a great degree
6. blight (157) – any cause of impairment, destruction, ruin, or frustration; affliction
7. precarious (164) – exposed to or involving danger; unsafe
8. profundity (165) – great depth; seriousness
9. impotence (166) – lack of self-restraint; powerlessness
10. inexorable (167) – unable to be persuaded, moved, or affected by entreaties; relentless

Chapters Twenty–One–Twenty–Three
1. supposition (173) – assumption; hypothesis
2. languid (176) – lacking in vigor or vitality
3. visage (177) – the face, usually with reference to shape, features, or expression
4. vexations (180) – irritations; annoyances
5. degradation (183) – lowered in dignity, character, or rank
6. imperious (184) – intensely compelling
7. vanquished (186) – conquered or subdued by superior force
8. enunciation (187) – the act of clearly stating or declaring something
9. artifice (190) – the use of trickery; deception
10. reverie (191) – state of dreamy meditation or fanciful musing; daydream

Chapter Twenty–Four, Continuation
1. abjuration (200) – the act of renouncing or recanting one's errors
2. repast (201) – a meal
3. scoffing (202) – being derisive or scornful; mocking; jeering
4. procured (203) – obtained by care, effort, or special means
5. disencumbered (205) – freed from a burden
6. congeal (206) – to change from a soft or fluid state to a rigid or solid state, as by cooling or freezing
7. dispositions (209) – natural mental and emotional outlooks or moods
8. actuated (214) – incited or moved to action
9. superfluous (216) – unnecessary; needless
10. contumely (218) – contemptuous or humiliating treatment; insult

Frankenstein
Post-Reading Activities and Alternative Assessment

Cross-Curricular Activities (Multiple Subjects)
1. Research an Arctic explorer and his exploration. Create and perform a one-person narrative as the explorer.
2. Learn about alchemy and alchemists. Dress as an alchemist as you share the information you learn with the class.
3. Make a poster or brochure about the life of Mary Shelley. Include information about major events in her life, her major works, and how her life influenced her writing.

Social Science/ History
4. Learn about the importance of companionship to humans. Write a report outlining what you learn.
5. Investigate the American legal system and process of bringing someone to trial. Create a PowerPoint presentation outlining the American legal system and contrasting it to Justine's trial and conviction.
6. Investigate the British (or other) legal system and process of bringing someone to trial. Create a power point presentation outlining the legal system and contrasting it to Justine's trial and conviction.
7. Read about Maslow's Hierarchy of Needs. Write an essay explaining how the creature could have been more amenable to humans if his basic needs had been better met.
8. Research the process of learning to speak and read. Create a visual display explaining these processes and share it orally with the class.

Geography
9. Create detailed maps of at least two of the countries (Switzerland, Germany, Scotland, England) visited by Victor Frankenstein.
10. Research at least one of the countries (Switzerland, Germany, Scotland, England) visited by Victor Frankenstein. Create a visual display to share what you learn.

Science
11. Research all aspects of stem cell research. Create a visual display explaining your opinion regarding the pros and cons of stem cell research.
12. Learn about the history of natural science and chemistry. Create a timeline marking significant events and scientists of the discipline(s).
13. The DeLacey family depended on their garden to supply year-round food for their family. Create a plan for a year-round garden that would grow in your area. Be sure to include when you should plant, harvest, and rotate each crop.

Art/ Drama/ Music
14. Create a one-person play of a scene from *Frankenstein*. You may switch voices and use props to portray different characters. Memorize and rehearse your one-person show and perform it for the class.
15. With a classmate(s), reenact your favorite scene from the novel. Before you act out the scene, rewrite it into a play format and memorize your lines.
16. Select songs to form a soundtrack for *Frankenstein*. Think about what genre(s) of music would be most appropriate for the novel. Burn a CD of the soundtrack you have created. Include an explanation of when each song would occur in the novel and why you chose each song. Also include the name of each song, the group or artist performing the song, and the year the song was written. Make a creative CD case with a picture that relates to the novel and include a listing of the song titles of the back cover.

Frankenstein
Essay/Writing Ideas

For this Guide, essay and writing activities are two different types of writing assignments. For the essay ideas, be sure to answer the questions in a succinct, comprehensive, minimum five-paragraph essay. Each answer should be at least 2-3 typed, double-spaced pages.

Below the Essay Ideas are writing activities that do not necessarily follow the "essay" format. For the writing ideas, follow the directions as given.

Essay Ideas

1. Write an essay discussing what Victor learns throughout the course of the novel. How do his goals and plans change as the novel progresses?

2. Write an essay delineating how Mary Shelley creates a Gothic mood and tone in the novel. Provide examples from the novel to support your assertions.

3. Analyze a character other than Victor Frankenstein or the creature. What is his/her role in the story? Is he/she necessary to the novel? Why or why not?

4. In your opinion, discuss how Victor Frankenstein could have helped the creature acclimate to and be accepted by society. What would you have done differently?

5. Write an essay explaining how the creature of Frankenstein forms the archetypal horror character.

6. Evaluate literary Romanticism and discuss how the Romantic ideals extend through 20th and 21st century literature.

7. Evaluate Victor's actions from an ethical point of view. How does Victor act or shy away from acting ethically?

8. Compare the creature's development and actions to those of a child. Does viewing the creature as a child alter one's view of him? Why or why not?

9. Evaluate *Frankenstein* in terms of its message regarding women's rights in its historical era. Which characters further this cause and which detract from it? Explain the reasons for your answer.

10. Compare and contrast *Frankenstein* to *Paradise Lost* and the myth of Prometheus.

11. Read one or more of the novels (*Plutarch's Lives*, Goethe's *The Sorrows of Werter*, Milton's *Paradise Lost*) that the creature read. Evaluate the effect the narrative had on the creature's character.

Writing Ideas

1. Watch a movie version of *Frankenstein*. Write an essay comparing and contrasting the movie and the novel.

2. Read one or more of the novels (*Plutarch's Lives*, Goethe's *The Sorrows of Werter*, Milton's *Paradise Lost*) that the creature read. Write a summary of the book(s).

3. Write a sequel to *Frankenstein*. Include what you believe happens to the creature and Robert Walton.

4. Write a new ending to *Frankenstein*. Include how the novel would have concluded differently if Victor had created a female mate for the creature.

5. Write a modern-day version of the novel in which the creature is derived from a cloning experiment gone awry.

6. Write several entries of Victor Frankenstein's journal explaining how he formed and created his monster.

7. Victor states, "In other studies you go as far as others have gone before you, and there is nothing more to know; but in a scientific pursuit there is continual food for discovery and wonder." (48) In light of this comment, trace a modern-day scientific discovery or tenet back through history. Show how each scientist built on the work of his/her predecessors.

8. Mary Shelley wrote prose, and her husband wrote poetry. Select a poem about nature to rewrite in prose. Next, rewrite a descriptive passage of prose as a poem. Decide and explain if you think it is more challenging to write prose or poetry.

9. Rewrite Victor's decision not to create a female monster from the creature's point of view.

10. The letters reveal much of Victor and Elizabeth's relationship. Create and tell a story in a series of letters.

Project Rubric A

Category	Score of 5	Score of 4	Score of 3	Score of 2	Score of 1	Score
Required Elements	Includes all of the required elements as stated in the directions.	Includes all but one or two of the required elements as stated in the directions.	Missing 3 or 4 of the required elements as stated in the directions.	Missing 5 or 6 of the required elements as stated in the directions.	Project does not follow the directions.	
Graphics, Pictures	All pictures, drawings, or graphics are appropriate and add to the enjoyment of the project.	Some pictures, drawings, or graphics are included, are appropriate, and add to the enjoyment of the project.	A few pictures, drawings, or graphics are included and are appropriate to the project.	A few pictures, drawings, or graphics are included, but may not be appropriate to the project, or may be distracting.	Pictures or drawings are not used and/or are inappropriate or distracting to the project.	
Creativity	Exceptionally clever and unique; design and presentation enhance the project.	Clever at times; thoughtfully and uniquely presented.	A few original or clever touches enhance the project.	Little evidence of uniqueness, individuality, and/or effort.	No evidence of creativity or effort. Project is not unique.	
Neatness, Appeal	Exceptionally neat and attractive; typed or very neatly hand-written, appropriate use of color, particularly neat in design and layout.	Neat and attractive; typed or neatly handwritten, good use of color, good design and layout.	Generally neat and attractive; handwritten, some use of color, some problems in design and layout.	Distractingly messy or disorganized; handwritten; little use of color; several problems in design and layout.	Work shows no pride or effort. Project is incomplete, illegible, or particularly messy and unattractive.	
Grammar, Spelling, Mechanics	Little to no problems with grammar, spelling, and mechanics. Project was clearly proofread.	A few problems with grammar, spelling, or mechanics. Errors are minor and do not distract from the project.	Several errors in grammar, spelling, or mechanics. Errors can be slightly distracting at times.	Several problems with grammar, spelling, or mechanics. Errors are distracting.	Many problems with grammar, spelling, or mechanics. Mistakes clearly show project was not proofread.	

Comments:

Final Score: _____ out of 25

Project Rubric B

Category	Score of 5	Score of 4	Score of 3	Score of 2	Score of 1	Score
Required Elements	Includes all of the required elements as stated in the directions.	Includes all but one or two of the required elements as stated in the directions.	Missing 3 or 4 of the required elements as stated in the directions.	Missing 5 or 6 of the required elements as stated in the directions.	Project does not follow the directions.	
Creativity	Exceptionally clever and unique; design and presentation enhance the project.	Clever at times; thoughtfully and uniquely presented.	A few original or clever touches enhance the project.	Little evidence of uniqueness, individuality, and/or effort.	No evidence of creativity or effort. Project is not unique.	
Neatness, Appeal	Exceptionally neat and attractive; typed or very neatly hand-written, appropriate use of color, particularly neat in design and layout.	Neat and attractive; typed or neatly handwritten, good use of color, good design and layout.	Generally neat and attractive; handwritten, some use of color, some problems in design and layout.	Distractingly messy or disorganized; handwritten; little use of color; several problems in design and layout.	Work shows no pride or effort. Project is incomplete, illegible, or particularly messy and unattractive.	
Grammar, Spelling, Mechanics	Little to no problems with grammar, spelling, and mechanics. Project was clearly proofread.	A few problems with grammar, spelling, or mechanics. Errors are minor and do not distract from the project.	Several errors in grammar, spelling, or mechanics. Errors can be slightly distracting at times.	Several problems with grammar, spelling, or mechanics. Errors are distracting.	Many problems with grammar, spelling, or mechanics. Mistakes clearly show project was not proofread.	
Citation of Sources	All graphics, pictures, and written work are original, or if they have been obtained from an outside source, have been properly cited.	All graphics, pictures, and written work that are not original or have been obtained from an outside source have been cited, with a few problems.	All graphics, pictures, and written work that are not original or have been obtained from an outside source have been cited, with several problems.	Some attempt has been made to give credit for unoriginal graphics, pictures, and written work.	No attempt has been made to give credit for unoriginal graphics, pictures, and written work.	

Comments:

Final Score: _____ out of 25

Response to Literature Rubric

Adapted from the **California Writing Assessment Rubric**
California Department of Education, Standards and Assessment Division

Score of 4
- ☐ Clearly addresses all parts of the writing task.
- ☐ Provides a meaningful thesis and thoughtfully supports the thesis and main ideas with facts, details, and/or explanations.
- ☐ Maintains a consistent tone and focus and a clear sense of purpose and audience.
- ☐ Illustrates control in organization, including effective use of transitions.
- ☐ Provides a variety of sentence types and uses precise, descriptive language.
- ☐ Contains few, if any, errors in the conventions of the English language (grammar, punctuation, capitalization, spelling). These errors do not interfere with the reader's understanding of the writing.
- ☐ Demonstrates a *clear* understanding of the ambiguities, nuances, and complexities of the text.
- ☐ Develops interpretations that demonstrate a thoughtful, comprehensive, insightful grasp of the text, and supports these judgments with specific references to various texts.
- ☐ Draws well-supported inferences about the effects of a literary work on its audience.
- ☐ Provides *specific* textual examples and/or personal knowledge and details to support the interpretations and inferences.

Score of 3
- ☐ Addresses all parts of the writing task.
- ☐ Provides a thesis and supports the thesis and main ideas with mostly relevant facts, details, and/or explanations.
- ☐ Maintains a generally consistent tone and focus and a general sense of purpose and audience.
- ☐ Illustrates control in organization, including *some* use of transitions.
- ☐ Includes a variety of sentence types and *some* descriptive language.
- ☐ Contains some errors in the conventions of the English language. These errors do not interfere with the reader's understanding of the writing.
- ☐ Develops interpretations that demonstrate a comprehensive grasp of the text and supports these interpretations with references to various texts.
- ☐ Draws supported inferences about the effects of a literary work on its audience.
- ☐ Supports judgments with some specific references to various texts and/or personal knowledge.
- ☐ Provides textual examples and details to support the interpretations.

Score of 2

- ☐ Addresses *only parts* of the writing task.
- ☐ *Suggests* a central idea with *limited* facts, details, and/or explanation.
- ☐ Demonstrates *little* understanding of purpose and audience.
- ☐ Maintains an *inconsistent* point of view, focus, and/or organizational structure which may include *ineffective or awkward* transitions that do not unify important ideas.
- ☐ Contains *several errors* in the conventions of the English language. These errors may interfere with the reader's understanding of the writing.
- ☐ Develops interpretations that demonstrate a limited grasp of the text.
- ☐ Includes interpretations that *lack* accuracy or coherence as related to ideas, premises, or images from the literary work.
- ☐ Draws *few* inferences about the effects of a literary work on its audience.
- ☐ Supports judgments with *few, if any*, references to various text and/or personal knowledge.

Score of 1

- ☐ Addresses *only one* part of the writing task.
- ☐ *Lacks* a thesis or central idea but may contain *marginally related* facts, details, and/or explanations.
- ☐ Demonstrates *no* understanding of purpose and audience.
- ☐ *Lacks* a clear point of view, focus, organizational structure, and transitions that unify important ideas.
- ☐ Includes *no* sentence variety; sentences are simple.
- ☐ Contains *serious errors* in the conventions of the English language. These errors interfere with the reader's understanding of the writing.
- ☐ Develops interpretations that demonstrate *little* grasp of the text.
- ☐ *Lacks* an interpretation or *may* be a simple retelling of the text.
- ☐ *Lacks* inferences about the effects of a literary work on its audience.
- ☐ *Fails* to support judgments with references to various text and/or personal knowledge.
- ☐ *Lacks* textual examples and details.

Answer Key

Note: Answers may not be given in complete sentences, as most student answers should be.

Page 7: Pre-Reading Activity: Biological Scientific Research

Answers will vary. Sample answers are given.

1. a. Allows couples with fertility issues to have families.
    b. High rate of multiple births and medical problems experienced by multiples; some people may argue on religious beliefs that in vitro allows non-traditional families to have children; fewer people adopt children since they are able to give birth to their own

2. a. Treat genetic conditions; grow new organs to replace damaged ones which would minimize the need for organ donors; clone endangered animals
    b. Some people may argue on religious grounds that cloning takes the place of a higher being who should be the only one to create life; use to clone dangerous animals or people (in the future); minimal regulation of scientific process; potential for something to go wrong in the process, creating a new disease or other.

3. a. Stem cells could be used to grow new organs to replace a person's damaged tissue or organ, eliminating the need for an external donor; studying stem cells may give scientists insight into birth defects and diseases such as cancer, Parkinson's disease, etc.
    b. Using embryonic stem cells often requires destroying the embryo from which the cells were harvested. To some, this is equivalent to abortion.

4. a. By isolating genes that cause birth defects, the birth defects could be eliminated; chronic diseases such as heart disease and asthma may be eliminated; we could create "super" babies who do certain jobs in society
    b. Parents may try to make designer babies with specific hair color and other traits; only a higher being should engage in the process of making human beings with specific characteristics; by creating a "super" baby, Carried to its extreme, there would be no lower-level people—those who engage in blue-collar type jobs—everyone would be too "intelligent", too "athletic," or too "beautiful"

Page 11: Comprehension Check: Exploring Expository Writing—Author Biography

1. As a child, Mary was surrounded by the literary giants and progressive thinkers who associated with her father, William Godwin. Aside from being exposed to the authors' ideas and works, Mary met Percy Bysshe Shelley when he visited her father. Her relationship with Percy impacted and influenced Mary from the time she was sixteen.

2. Mary and Percy's out-of-wedlock relationship would have been looked down on in nineteenth century society. The fact that Percy Shelley was married and continued a sexual relationship with his wife makes Percy's relationship with Mary even more scandalous. Percy's atheistic beliefs show that he is not concerned with being received by traditional society or with being subjected to traditional beliefs and behaviors. Mary's non-traditional upbringing also makes her more willing to embrace a scandalous relationship with Percy Shelley.

3. Percy Shelley's relationship with Lord Byron created the opportunity and reason for Mary to begin writing *Frankenstein*. Percy also acted as Mary's editor and mentor.

4. *Answers may vary. Sample answer:* At that time, it would have been unthinkable for a woman to write a horror tale; people would not believe that an eighteen-year-old could have written the novel. Many people assumed that Percy Shelley wrote *Frankenstein*.

5. *Frankenstein* in 1818, *Valperga* in 1823, *The Last Man* in 1826, *The Fortunes of Perkin Warbeck* in 1830, *Falkner* in 1837

Page 13: Standards Focus: Exploring Expository Writing—Genre

1. nature, travel, folklore, and legends

2. Sixteen-year-old Mary Godwin and the married Percy Shelley's journey through Europe and Mary's out-of-wedlock pregnancy exemplified the Romantics' rebellion against conservative morality.

3. Victor Frankenstein's experiments, dark and secretive search for body parts in graves, spooky, faraway settings; a supernatural Frankenstein.

4. *Answers will vary. Sample answer:* the *Twilight* or *Vampire Diaries* series, both of which utilize supernatural characters that exist in a shadowy world.

5. scientific principles and modern technology

6. *Answers will vary*, but students should discuss how the book/movie uses scientific principles and modern technology.

Page 15: Standards Focus: Mythology

1. Prometheus created humans from clay and gave fire to humans.
2. While Mary Shelley spent the summer with Byron and Percy Shelley, Byron wrote a poem entitled "Prometheus" and Percy Shelley planned to write a rebuttal to Aeschylus's play *Prometheus Bound.*
3. William Blake alluded to Prometheus in the illustrations for "Visions of the Daughters of Albion" and Goethe wrote a verse drama entitled *Prometheus.*
4. Mary Shelley names the main character Victor after the penname used by Percy Shelley.
5. Victor Frankenstein creates the monster out of inanimate parts, and he uses lightning to bring his monster to life.
6. *Answers will vary*, but students should refer to specific characters and elements of Greek mythology.

Page 23: Note-Taking and Summarizing: Letters

Each set of chapters has at least one page for this activity. See *Summary of the Novel* (pp. 127-129) for possible answers. *Student answers will always vary.*

Page 24: Prologue, Letters: Comprehension Check

Prologue

1. Although it is in the voice and persona of Mary, it was said to be written by Percy Bysshe Shelley, Mary Shelley's husband; publishers wanted to know the origin of the novel, and how a young girl could come up with such a hideous story
2. *The History of the Inconstant Lover,* in which a man marries a ghost; the tale of the "sinful founder of his race" who gave the kiss of death on all young men, who quickly withered away to death
3. That evening, they talked of Darwin, who, it was said, animated a piece of vermicelli in a jar. They talked of reanimation of the dead, and the possibility of giving life to lifeless or inanimate objects.
4. *Answers will vary. Sample answer: Frankenstein* is really a tale about human passions—it "affords a point of view to the imagination for the delineating of human passions."
5. The *Iliad*, the tragic poetry of Greece; Shakespeare's *Tempest* and *Midsummer Night's Dream*; and Milton's *Paradise Lost*
6. In the summer of 1816 in Geneva, Switzerland, Mary Shelley began writing *Frankenstein* as part of a ghost story writing contest with several friends. It was started as a mode of entertainment, and partly for using that part of the mind which rarely gets used.

Letters

1. The letters set a context for the story within the larger world. The letters also generate curiosity in the reader regarding who boarded the ship and who he was following.
2. Romanticism dealt with the themes of adventure and travel (Walton exploring the Arctic) to educate one's self (Walton's attempt at self-education).
3. Walton went on whaling expeditions in the North Sea and worked on a Greenland whaler. He also studied math, medicine, and physical science.
4. *Answers will vary.* Walton most likely only has passable chances for a successful voyage. He seems to have jumped into being an explorer without extensive preparation or training. He may experience problems with his ship, managing the crew, navigation, fuel, ice floes, etc.
5. a friend
6. Due to his time spent in solitude and with his sister, Walton does not approve of brutality. The master of his ship is particularly courageous and honorable, but leads his ship without the usual brutality connected with such a position.
7. Helping the couple who are truly in love and not marrying for money adheres to the Romantic ideals of following emotion rather than reason.
8. Frankenstein's story involves the creation of a "marvelous," not-completely-human being who came to exist by forces other than nature or the "natural."
9. The fourth letter occurs in a far-away locale (Arctic), as a ship is eerily surrounded by a dense fog and ice floes—giving a sense of the unknown, danger, and mystery.
10. The sailors first see a gigantic man in a sledge led by dogs.
11. The man who boards the ship is haggard and in poor health. He is well-spoken and of European descent. He speaks English with an accent.
12. The man is "seeking one who fled from me."
13. The man becomes the friend that Walton so desperately wanted
14. The man agrees to tell Walton his story as a warning of becoming obsessed over seeking knowledge, but also so he can relieve himself of his burden and guilt.

15. The speaker's search for knowledge and wisdom brought him only pain, misery, and trouble.
16. to take notes on the man's story

Pages 25-27: Standards Focus: Mood and Tone
Answers will vary. Sample answers are given.
1.
    a. makes the novel seem more important than just a ghost story; makes it appear as if the story will teach us a lesson about life while entertaining us
    b. wants novel to be viewed in the tradition of great literature
    c. feelings shown in novel apply across the human condition
    d. sets up novel as creepy and eerie, helping contribute to the Gothic nature of the story
2. *Answers will vary*, but should include that the author wants the novel to be taken seriously, not just seen as an amusing ghost story. The novel speaks to all of humanity, not just the particular instance in the novel.
3. *Passages will vary. Sample answers:* "I desire the company... eyes would reply to mine." – reader feels sorry for Walton; "How would such... your poor brother."- portrays friendship as the cure for Walton's feelings; "I greatly need... regulate my mind."- shows the importance of companionship for humans; "there is a love for the marvelous... I am about to explore."- Walton's willingness to accept the marvelous makes him a willing listener for Frankenstein's story
4. *Answers will vary*, but should include that the author wants the reader to feel sorry for Walton and his loneliness; with the indications given, Shelley also wants us to recognize the loneliness we have felt as a universal feeling, making us more sympathetic of both Walton and Frankenstein, and eventually, Frankenstein's monster
5. "compassed round by a very thick fog"- creepy setting; "we beheld... seemed to have no end."- frightening scene; "We perceived... the dogs."- brings Frankenstein's story into the eerie scene; "fearing to encounter... breaking up of the ice."- introduces fear into the story; "It was, in fact, a sledge... but a European."- evokes curiosity in the reader.
6. *Answers will vary*, but should include that the precarious situation of the ship and the eerie setting create the scene for a creepy ghost story

Pages 28-29: Assessment Preparation: Vocabulary in Context
Students' definitions and sentences will vary. Part b. Dictionary Definitions are given.
1. explaining; describing or outlining in detail
2. method; resource; a means to an end
3. bad omens; strong inner feelings of a future misfortune or evil
4. satisfy; to gratify to the fullest
5. temptation; something that leads one forward with desire or hope
6. characteristics; attributes of mind or body
7. attention; concern for someone or something
8. face; look or expression of the face
9. sad; a gloomy state of mind

Page 30: Chapters One—Two: Note-Taking and Summarizing
Each chapter or set of chapters has at least one page for this activity. See *Summary of the Novel* (pp. 127-129) for possible answers. Student answers will always vary.

Page 31: Chapters One—Two: Comprehension Check
Chapter One
1. Victor's father, Alphonse Frankenstein, helped a friend, Beaufort, who fell on hard times. After Beaufort died, Victor cared for and eventually married Beaufort's daughter, Caroline.
2. Alphonse Frankenstein cares for Beaufort when he becomes poor. Caroline regularly visits and helps the poor. Elizabeth is adopted from a poor family who can no longer care for her.
3. Caroline and Elizabeth are both portrayed as virtuous women who are rescued, cared for, and protected by men. Elizabeth is also presented to Victor as a gift.
4. Victor enjoys an idyllic childhood and is doted on by his parents as they travel throughout Europe.
5. When visiting the poor, Caroline meets a peasant family who has taken in Elizabeth from a Milanese nobleman. The family can no longer afford to care for Elizabeth, so the Frankensteins adopt her.
6. Victor adores Elizabeth and feels that she is "mine to protect, love, and cherish" and that she is "my more than sister, since till death she was to be mine only." *(This foreshadows Elizabeth's death on her wedding-night.)*

Chapter Two

1. Victor tends to avoid crowds and instead, forms close friendships with only a few people—mostly one—Henry Clerval.

2. Victor desires to learn about science—the secrets of heaven and earth, and the "inner spirit of nature" and the "physical secrets of the world," while Henry Clerval prefers the "moral relations" of things, including history and literature.

3. While Victor's interest in science begins as an innocent search for knowledge, it grows to overwhelm and eventually destroy him and everything he loves.

4. Victor becomes obsessed with reading the works of early alchemists (Cornelius Agrippa, Paracelsus, and Albertus Magnus). An interest in alchemy then proceeds to an interest in natural science.

5. Victor educates himself in alchemy and natural science. This reflects a Romantic focus on self-education and parallels Robert Walton educating himself about sailing and the world.

6. When he was about 15 years old, Victor saw a lightning bolt destroy a tree and wondered about the power of lightning and electricity. *(This foreshadows Victor using lightning to bring his creature to life.)*; For a fleeting moment, Victor decided to abandon all of his ideas of natural science and alchemy, and his quest for "would-be" science for the sake of science based upon a "secure foundation." However, this did not last long, and "destiny" took over.

7. Victor feels that his destiny was to study the science of the unknown: "It was a strong effort of the spirit of good; but it was ineffectual. Destiny was too potent, and her immutable laws had decreed my utter and terrible destruction." (39)

Pages 32-33: Standards Focus: Character Interactions
Answers will vary. Sample answers are given.

1. Adopted from a peasant family who was caring for her (30); daughter of a Milanese nobleman and German mother (30); angelic appearance (31); presented to Victor as a gift (31); calm and virtuous (33); adored by Victor and entire family (34); same age as Victor (33); soothes Victor with her gentleness (35)

2. Doted on by his well-to-do parents (29); solitary, tends to isolate himself (33); obsessed with learning about the sciences (34); interested in alchemy (36); educated himself about natural science (37); interested in the power of lightning and electricity (37-38)

3. Students' responses should present Elizabeth and Victor as opposites. Elizabeth's gentle personality helps soothe and mitigate Victor's surly, obsessive tendencies.

Pages 34-35: Assessment Preparation: Spelling, Punctuation, and Capitalization
Answers, especially punctuation, may vary.

1. He came like a protecting spirit to the poor girl, who committed herself to his care; and after the interment of his friend, he conducted her to Geneva, and placed her under the protection of a relation.

2. There was a show of gratitude and worship in his attachment to my mother, differing wholly from the doating fondness of age, for it was inspired by reverence for her virtues, and a desire to be the means of, in some degree, recompensing her for the sorrows she had endured, but which gave inexpressible grace to his behavior to her. (The modern spelling of doating is doting: to dote.)

3. During one of their walks a poor cot in the folding of a vale attracted their notice as being singularly disconsolate, while the number of half-clothed children gathered about it spoke of penury in its worst shape.

4. The passionate and almost reverential attachment with which all regarded her became, while I shared it, my pride and my delight.

5. My temper was sometimes violent, and my passions vehement; but by some law in my temperature they were turned, not towards childish pursuits, but to an eager desire to learn, and not to learn all things indiscriminately.

6. I also record those events which led, by insensible steps, to my after tale of misery: for when I would account to myself for the birth of that passion, which afterwards ruled my destiny, I find it arise, like a mountain river, from ignoble and almost forgotten sources; but, swelling as it proceeded, it became the torrent which, in its course, has swept away all my hopes and joys.

7. If, instead of this remark, my father had taken the pains to explain to me that the principles of Agrippa had been entirely exploded, and that a modern system of science had been introduced, which possessed much greater powers than the ancient, because the powers of the latter were chimerical, while those of the former were real and practical. . . .

8. He might dissect, anatomize, and give names; but, not to speak of a final cause, causes in their secondary and tertiary grades were utterly unknown to him.
9. It was a strong effort of the spirit of good; but it was ineffectual.

Page 37: Chapters Three—Five: Note-Taking and Summarizing
Each set of chapters has at least one page for this activity. See *Summary of the Novel* (pp. 127-129) for possible answers. *Student answers will always vary.*

Page 38: Chapters Three—Five: Comprehension Check
Chapter Three
1. Caroline Frankenstein hopes that Elizabeth and Victor marry each other.
2. Elizabeth becomes the family's maternal figure. Rather than grieving, she devotes herself to caring for the family.
3. Henry's father does not see the point in education, and wants Henry to follow his footsteps in the world of commerce and trade.
4. Victor is destined for evil—his destiny was to have the Angel of Destruction decide his future.
5. Victor finds M. Krempe to be conceited and condescending. Victor likes M. Waldman much better, and respects him. It was his lecture that prompted Victor to keep searching for answers and keep moving forward, looking to be a leader in his profession—leading to his creation. M. Waldman becomes his mentor.

Chapter Four
1. *Answers will vary.* Victor means that many pursuits offer an ending point of knowledge. When learning a new skill, a point exists at which one has mastered it. When researching a social science or historical topic, one can reach a saturation point at which one has read most of the research on a topic. In science, an ending point does not exist, however, because there is always more to learn and explore.
2. Victor studies human anatomy, how life is created, death, and decay.
3. Victor thinks his creation will be grateful to and appreciative of him, like both a father and great Creator.
4. Victor becomes obsessed with science and his creation. It dominates his life at the expense of his health, family, and mental health.

5. Victor knows that he is doing something wrong and isolates himself from others so they will not learn of his actions.

Chapter Five
1. Victor is disgusted and runs screaming from the room. (55) *Answers will vary. Sample answer:* I was totally surprised at his reaction. I expected him to at least check out his creation, to take some time with it to see how all of his work came out.
2. Victor dreams that he sees and kisses Elizabeth. Elizabeth then changes to his dead mother who rots in his arms.
3. Like the mariner, Victor feels fear that he is being followed by the monster.
4. Victor is thrilled to see Henry Clerval. After acting erratically, jumping on furniture and running around in excitement, Victor collapses in a fit.
5. *Answers will vary*, but should include specific, realistic details. *Sample answer:* The monster fleas from the laboratory and wanders aimlessly in the countryside surrounding the town. During that time, the monster begins to learn about his senses and how his body functions.
6. Henry asks Victor to write a letter to his father and Elizabeth.

Pages 39-40: Standards Focus: Literary Archetypes
Answers will vary. Sample answers are given.
1. a. Elizabeth is repeatedly portrayed as putting others' desires and feelings before her own. She stays in the background and quietly, gratefully, and happily cares for others.
   b. *Answers will vary.* Some may argue Desdemona in *Othello*, Lenina in *Brave New World*, Ophelia in *Hamlet*. Students may have a difficult time with this. Discuss why coming up with the portrayal of weak, passive women in Literature is more difficult today. (The rejection of these roles beginning with Jane Austin and Charlotte Bronte).
2. a. Victor makes a living being by himself. He anticipates only positives occurring from his creation.
   b. *Answers will vary.* Be sure to discuss the Prometheus myth.
3. a. Victor uses parts of corpses to create his being. He gathers these pieces by combing through graves and morgues.
   b. *Answers will vary.* Some students may argue Doctor Emmett "Doc" Brown in the *Back to the Future* series, Faust in *Dr.*

Faustus, Lex Luthor (Superman's nemesis), Dr. Evil in the *Austin Powers* movies

4. a. The monster has a grotesque appearance. Shelley only alludes to bringing the monster to life with lightning when she says "infuse a spark of being," but movies frequently portray the monster's creation during a lightning storm. The monster leaves the lab on his own accord to wreck havoc in the world.

    b. *Answers will vary.* Be sure to discuss the archetypal monsters such as vampires, werewolves, etc.

    c. *Answers will vary.* If time allows, students may enjoy watching the creation scene in a variety of Frankenstein movies.

    d. Some students may have been surprised to learn that Frankenstein is not the monster himself, but the man who created the monster. This misconception is found throughout pop-culture and is perpetuated in movies and television.

Page 42-43: Assessment Preparation: Vocabulary in Context

Inferences and context clues will vary. Part of Speech, Word Root, and Definitions have been given.

1. repose: clues—akin to death
    a. noun; pose
    b. quiet place
    c. peace; state of restfulness or calm
2. repugnance: clues—secluded; domestic
    a. noun; repugnant
    b. opposition
    c. strong distaste, aversion, or objection
3. reprobated: clues—useless
    a. verb; reprobate
    b. disliked
    c. disapproved or condemned
4. recapitulation: clues—began his lecture
    a. noun; capitulate
    b. review
    c. restatement; a brief review or summary
5. deference: clues—due from a youth to his instructor
    a. noun; defer
    b. respect
    c. admiration; respectful or courteous regard
6. dogmatism: clues—gentleness was never tinged by
    a. noun; dogma
    b. obnoxiousness
    c. stubbornness; arrogant assertions of one's opinions as truths
7. hinderance (hindrance): clues—minuteness of the parts formed

    a. noun; hinder
    b. problem
    c. obstacle; something that interferes or delays action or progress
8. incipient: clues—would then drive away
    a. adjective; incipient
    b. deadly
    c. new; budding; beginning to exist or appear
9. languor: clues—extreme weakness
    a. noun; languor
    b. exhaustion
    c. lethargy; lack of energy or vitality

Page 44: Chapters Six—Eight: Note-Taking and Summarizing

Each set of chapters has at least one page for this activity. See *Summary of the Novel* (pp. 127-129) for possible answers. *Student answers will always vary.*

Page 45: Chapters Six—Eight: Comprehension Check
Chapter Six

1. Elizabeth writes that she is regretful that she was not there to take care of Victor when he was so sick; that his father is doing well; Ernest is now sixteen and wants to enter the military; the story of how Justine joined the family; of little William and his new girlfriend of five years old; some gossip of the town
2. At age 12, Justine lives with the Frankensteins after her own mother mistreats her. When her mother later becomes sick, Justine leaves the Frankensteins to care for her mother, but returns after her mother passes away.
3. William, the youngest Frankenstein child, has blue eyes, curly hair, and dark eyelashes. He has dimples and is a happy child. He seems to be between 7 and 10 years old.
4. Victor realizes that his lack of communication with his family has caused them pain and anxiety; he immediately exhausts himself writing a letter to them.
5. M. Waldman and M. Krempe both praise Victor and his knowledge of science. Both of these men commend Victor on his studies—in his pursuit of knowledge and talents as a student—and infer that he has the potential to do great things. The irony is that Victor used this knowledge and these talents to create a monster that would eventually destroy him.
6. Victor and Clerval begin studying the Asian languages of Persian, Arabic, and Sanskrit.

7. Through his companionship and attentiveness, Clerval lifts Victor's mood and gets him back to feeling like a normal person and his old self.

Chapter Seven

1. William was either strangled or his neck was broken—a fingerprint was found on his neck.
2. She gave William a locket with his mother's picture to wear around his neck—she thinks it was what the murderer wanted.
3. nearly six years
4. During the day, Victor describes the mountains as placid and welcoming. At night, he feels they are dark and gloomy, and a scene of evil.
5. Lightning "plays on the summit of Mont Blanc" and flashes about the Alps of Savoy illuminating the lake at its base. A flash of lightning also illuminates the creature in the distance.
6. He hesitates at first because the monster was escaping too quickly. He then second-guesses whether he should tell his story because he convinces himself that no one would believe him, and they would think he had gone insane. He then reassures himself that even if he told his story, the monster would have been able to escape before they could even begin hunting him down. Finally, he wonders who would be strong enough to capture him.
7. *Answers will vary*, but should include details to support the response. *Sample answer:* If William had been with Victor, the monster may have pursued Victor instead of the child. If the monster truly wanted to punish Victor by killing his brother, Victor would probably have been powerless to prevent it, though.
8. Victor mistakenly believes that his family knows that the monster killed William, and that they have captured the monster.
9. The locket containing the picture of Caroline Frankenstein is found in Justine's pocket.
10. She trusts Justine and considers her a part of the family that she knows really well. She firmly believes she knows Justine is incapable of committing such a crime, especially against William.

Chapter Eight

1. Since he was not in town at the time of the murder, Victor believes that he will be viewed as a madman if he tells who he believes murdered William.
2. Justine provides contradictory answers to questions, cannot account for her whereabouts, and does not know how the locket got in her pocket.

3. Justine does not have any enemies, and believes that her character and behavior to this point in her life will set her free. She cannot fathom someone (or something) so evil as to deliberately destroy her.
4. Elizabeth says that Justine acted as a mother to William and would not have hurt him. Elizabeth also says that Justine would not have needed to steal the locket since she would have given it to Justine if she had asked for it.
5. He states that he is worse off than Justine because she knows she is innocent, and he is plagued by guilt and remorse because he knows he is responsible.
6. *Answers will vary*, but without the confession Justine may not have been convicted. The judge does tell Elizabeth and Victor "indeed, none of our judges like to condemn a criminal upon circumstantial evidence, be it ever so decisive."
7. She was hoping to be absolved and to be saved; she was forced into it out of fear of hell and eternal damnation.
8. *Answers will vary*. By keeping his suspicions regarding the monster to himself, Victor allows Justine to take the blame for William's murder. Doing so also allows Victor to keep his monster a secret, as well as avoid anyone thinking that he is mentally unstable for suggesting the existence of a monster which no one has seen.
9. Justine is not provided a lawyer. She is convicted on circumstantial evidence. She does not receive a trial by jury. She is bullied into a confession. She is immediately executed and not allowed time for an appeal.

Pages 46-47: Standards Focus: Imagery
Answers will vary. Sample answers have been provided.
Sight: "I discovered more distinctly the black sides of Jura, and the bright summit of Mont Blanc." (p. 73, par. 2); "Your summits are clear; the sky and lake are blue and placid. Is this to prognosticate peace, or to mock at my unhappiness?" (p. 73, par. 2); "Night also closed around; and when I could hardly see the dark mountains, I felt still more gloomily." (p. 73, par. 4); ". . . vivid flashes of lightning dazzled my eyes, illuminating the lake making it appear like a vast sheet of fire. . ." (p. 74, par. 2); "A flash of lightning illuminated the object, and discovered its shape plainly to me; its gigantic stature, and the deformity of its aspect, more hideous than belongs to humanity, instantly informed me that is was

the wretch, the filthy demon, to whom I had given life." (p. 75, line 2);

Sound: ". . . the thunder burst with a terrific crash over my head. It was echoed from Saleve, the Juras, and the Alps of Savoy. . ." (p. 74, par. 2); "The thunder ceased; but the rain still continued, and the scene was enveloped in an impenetrable darkness."
(p. 75, par. 1)

Touch: "It advanced; the heavens were clouded, and I soon felt the rain coming slowly in large drops, but its violence quickly increased." (p. 74, par. 1); "No one can conceive the anguish I suffered during the remainder of the night, which I spent, cold and wet, in the open air." (p. 75, par. 2)

Emotions: "I hardly sustain the multitude of feelings that crowded into my mind. I passed through scenes familiar to my youth, but which I had not seen for nearly six years." (p. 73, line 3); "By degrees the calm and heavenly scene restored me, and I continued my journey towards Geneva." (p. 73, par. 1); "Night also closed around; and when I could hardly see the dark mountains, I felt still more gloomily." (p. 73, par. 4); "This noble war in the sky elevated my spirits; I clasped my hands, and exclaimed aloud, 'William, dear angel! This is thy funeral, this thy dirge!'" (p. 74, par. 3)

Answers will vary, but should compare how Victor's mood changes with how he perceives the landscape and its changes as night falls.

Pages 48-49: Assessment Preparation: Tenses of Verbs

1. is; remind
2. was; gave
3. said; is; intend
4. contemplated; were; was; were (not) changed
5. elevated; clasped; exclaimed; is
6. remembered; had been seized; would give
7. do; replied; have discovered; valued
8. forced; has been; leaves; will be; will hear
9. was; possessed; obliterated

Page 50: Chapters Nine—Ten: Note-Taking and Summarizing

Each set of chapters has at least one page for this activity. See *Summary of the Novel* (pp. 127-129) for possible answers. *Student answers will always vary.*

Page 51: Chapters Nine—Ten: Comprehension Check
Chapter Nine

1. Victor becomes deeply depressed and extremely remorseful; he is unable to sleep and wants to be alone.
2. Victor takes the boat onto the lake and ponders suicide.
3. When Victor created the being, he sought to create life and dispel death. Now Victor only thinks of destroying the creature.
4. Victor created the being that murdered William. Since Justine was put to death for William's murder, his creation also led to the girl's death. By speaking up about his suspicions, Victor may have been able to prevent Justine's death.
5. *Answers will vary. Sample answer:* Percy Shelley's poem: purely descriptive, more vivid vocabulary, concentrates on the actions of nature; Mary Shelley's narrative: easier to understand, description interrupted by Victor's actions, provides a general sense of what one would view near Mont Blanc.

Chapter Ten

1. *Answers will vary. Sample answer:* "These sublime and magnificent scenes afforded me the greatest consolation that I was capable of receiving. They elevated me from all littleness of feeling; and although they did not remove my grief, they subdued and tranquillized it." (94); "The sight of the awful and majestic in nature had indeed always the effect of solemnizing my mind, and causing me to forget the passing cares of life." (95)
2. Shelley describes the setting as "desolate," similar to Victor's desire for solitude, and "melancholy," akin to the depression that Victor experiences. The storm growing in the valley foreshadows Victor's meeting with the creature.
3. *Answers will vary. Sample answer:* The poem discusses the constant change inherent in the human condition, just as Victor's impending visit with the creature heralds a great change in his life. Some may claim that "the only thing constant is change."
4. The creature tells Victor that he will leave everyone at peace if Victor complies with his conditions, but will continue to murder if Victor does not do as the creature desires. Later, he says "Make me happy, and I shall again be virtuous."
5. The creature says that he was originally benevolent and kind, but that humans' abhorrence and rejection caused him to become full of hatred and evil.
6. He was once good, but has been turned evil because he is miserably lonely.

7. *Answers will vary. Sample answer:* In his speech to Victor, the creature portrays himself as well-spoken, intelligent, and reasonable—all of which make the reader sympathetic towards the creature's plight. The creature seems to be asking something reasonable—that Frankenstein give him a chance and listen to his story.

8. *Answers will vary. Sample answer:* I believe the creature wants Frankenstein to perform "surgery" on him so that he will become less hideous and more physically acceptable to human beings, and therefore be accepted as a part of humanity.

Pages 53-54: Standards Focus: Foreshadowing
Answers will vary. Sample answers are given.

1. a. Victor feels the creature will commit a more heinous crime
   b. Creature will commit a more horrific crime than William's murder—possibly even killing Elizabeth or Victor himself.
   c. Victor knows that the creature is capable of committing murder, and even has a feeling that he will kill again.

2. a. Victor pursuing monster, Victor seeing monster again
   b. Victor will see the monster again, and he will follow the monster in an effort to kill him and avenge the killings.
   c. Victor feels that since he created the monster who murdered William and Justine, he must also end the monster's life to avenge their deaths.

3. a. Victor is concerned about the monster harming Elizabeth
   b. The monster will harm Elizabeth.
   c. In the past, the monster has harmed a member of the Frankenstein family to get back at Victor.

4. a. The monster threatens to harm Victor's friends and family
   b. The monster will murder another member of Victor's friends or family
   c. The monster has previously murdered a member of the Frankenstein family and is now giving an ultimatum that he will do so again if he is not satisfied.

5. a. The monster will defend himself against any attempt by Victor to harm him, and the monster is stronger than normal humans.
   b. Victor will attempt to kill the creature, but will not succeed
   c. Victor's anger toward the creature causes him to try to kill the being.

6. a. Only Victor can prevent more deaths, and the monster threatens to harm more people.

b. The monster will murder again if Victor does not do as he says.
   c. The monster has previously demonstrated that he will murder in revenge.

7. a. Victor believes that he should try to comply with the creature's desires
   b. Victor will comply with the creature's demands out of fear of future harm.
   c. Victor wants to protect his family and friends from the creature's wrath.

Pages 56-58: Assessment Preparation: Precise Word Choice
Answers will vary. Sample answers are given.

1. a. Replacement: dishonorable desertion
   b. "Dishonorable" does not carry the connotation of lack of morality and ethics that "base" does.

2. a. Replacement: minimize the recollection of the past
   b. "Efface" means to completely wipe out or eliminate, but minimizing the crime would still leave it open for comparison.

3. a. Replacement: cliff
   b. "Abyss" recalls a deep cavity from which there is no return, but a person could possibly survive and recover from falling off a cliff which may not be as steep or deep as an abyss.

4. a. Replacement: time from which I dated all my woe
   b. "Epoch" means a time period with a specific beginning, i.e Justine's death, but "time" recalls a more general time period

5. a. Replacement: pale lightnings
   b. "Pale" implies light in color, whereas "pallid" means light in color and weak in strength.

6. a. Replacement: ascent is steep, but the path is cut into continual and short windings
   b. "Steep" just implies a sharp incline, whereas "precipitous" also implies the danger of the trek of the incline.

7. a. Replacement: sight tremendous and loathsome
   b. "Loathsome" infers a great hatred, but "abhorred" infers a hatred and ugliness that is difficult to view.

8. a. Replacement: wickedly murdered
   b. "Wickedly" includes the cruelty of the murderous act, but "diabolically" also infers the premeditation involved in the murder.

9. a. Replacement: do not look down on me
   b. Victor not only looks down on the creature as less than human, he also has great contempt for him which is inferred in the use of the word "disdain."

Page 59: Chapters Eleven-Twelve: Note-Taking and Summarizing

Each set of chapters has at least one page for this activity. See *Summary of the Novel* (pp. 127-129) for possible answers. *Student answers will always vary.*

Page 60: Chapters Eleven—Twelve: Comprehension Check

Chapter Eleven

1. from the creature's point of view
2. The creature does not understand anything about his surroundings or his body. As he wanders in the forest, he gradually learns to utilize his senses, eat berries, and drink water.
3. The creature finds a small, abandoned fire and gets burned when he puts his hand in it. Through observation, he learns to maintain the fire by adding wood to it. He then uses the fire for heat and to cook food.
4. *Answers will vary. Sample answer:* At first, the creature does not understand how his body works or how to use it. He also does not understand how the world works or human relationships. He must learn these skills through trial and error and observation.
5. The creature learns that he is not wanted or liked by humans. He realizes that humans are only tolerant of people similar to themselves. He also experiences the cruelty of man.
6. The creature's decision to isolate himself from humans is understandable given the human reactions he has experienced.
7. The family consists of an elderly blind man, his son, and daughter. The son and daughter constantly work, while the father plays music. Each of the family members seems sad, but they are benevolent and warm to each other.

Chapter Twelve

1. The creature thinks the DeLaceys live luxuriously since they have shelter, fire, food, clothing, and each other. In reality, the DeLaceys work hard for everything they have, are in deep poverty, and struggle just to eat.
2. The creature stops eating the DeLaceys' food and begins cutting wood and placing it at their door each night.
3. The creature observes the DeLacey family for "several revolutions of the moon" or several months.
4. The creature learns about family relationships, kindness, speech, music, and reading by observing the family.
5. The creature thinks that if he can speak to humans, they will overlook his frightening appearance.

6. When Victor made the creature, he felt that he was forming a race of superior beings. Now the supposedly "superior" creature thinks that a family who most humans would look down on is truly superior.
7. *Answers will vary.* Be sure that students think through the possible reactions that the DeLaceys may have toward the creature and how the creature could minimize or use them to his advantage.

Pages 61-62: Standards Focus: Symbolism

Part One

1. creature perceives strong light (101)
2. creature walks on land and discovers water (101)
3. eats berries (101)
4. notices moon and sun (102)
5. enjoys songs of birds (102)
6. sees humans for the first time (104)

Part Two

Answers may vary. Sample answers are given.

1. Chapter 11: Creature discovers fire, burns his hand in it, then learns to use the fire for warmth and cooking food (103); fire can both harm and help
2. Chapter 7: Lightning illuminates the creature near the site of William's death; lightning illuminates the Victor's revelation that the creature killed William (74)
3. Chapter 5: It is implied that lightning brings the creature to life; lightning as a force of creation (55)
4. Chapter 2: By observing a tree that has been destroyed by lightning, Victor realizes lightning's power; Lightning sparks Victor's interest in the laws of electricity. (38)

Part Three

Answers may vary. Sample answers are given.

Chapter 12: The creature's spirits improve as he experiences spring; spring is a rebirth and renewal. (114)

Chapter 10: A storm occurs in the valley as Victor climbs the mountain; the storm symbolizes Victor's internal turmoil. (95)

Chapter 9: Victor spends time by himself sailing on the lake at night; represents Victor's isolation and desire for solitude. (89)

Chapter 5: Victor brings the creature to life on a dreary night; the creature's existence heralds woe and trouble for Victor. (55)

Paragraphs will vary. Students will benefit from discussing the symbolism as a class before writing their paragraphs. Students should use and expand upon the examples in their writing.

**Pages 63-64: Assessment Preparation:
Complements**

1. Subject: I; Verb: lamented; DO: loss
2. Subject: I; Verbs: passed, discovered; DOs: days, country
3. Subject: man; Verb: met; DO: her
4. Subject: it; Verb: was; PN: sight
5. Subjects: man, he, they; Verbs: had been, assumed, sat; PA: pensive; DO: air
6. Subject: family; Verbs: extinguished, retired; DO: lights
7. Subject: nothing; Verb: could exceed; Dos: love, respect
8. Subjects: I, attention, time; Verbs: was, explained; PA: unable; DO: appearances
9. Subjects: showers, warmth; Verb: altered; DO: aspect
10. Subjects: light, I; Verbs: became, sought; PA: oppressive; DO: place
11. Subjects: ideas, all; Verbs: occupied, was; DO: mind; PA: confused
12. Subjects: I, they; Verbs: collected, were, would burn; DO: branches; PA: wet
13. Subjects: hair, countenance, manners; Verb: won, enticed; DO: reverence, love

Page 65: Chapters Thirteen—Fourteen: Note-Taking and Summarizing

Each set of chapters has at least one page for this activity. See *Summary of the Novel* (pp. 127-129) for possible answers. *Student answers will always vary.*

Page 66: Chapters Thirteen—Fourteen: Comprehension Check
Chapter Thirteen

1. A stranger who doesn't speak French; later, we learn her name is Safie. *Answers will vary. Sample answer:* I am guessing that Safie is Felix's old girlfriend from long ago. I predict that they were supposed to be married, but were not able to, even though they were in love. She lift's Felix's mood because he still loves her and is so happy to see her again. This scenario seems to fit well into the idea of Romanticism.
2. By observing the family, the creature learns to speak as the family teaches Safie to speak and read French.
3. The creature only leaves his hovel during nighttime and stays away from villages and other areas inhabited by humans.
4. The creature learns that humans can be virtuous and vicious, kind, and evil. He learns about history, including the Romans and Christianity and how the original people of the Americas were forced out of their native land.

He also learns of the division of property, wealth and poverty, rank, descent, and nobility, leading him to conclude that humans value wealth and power.

5. He also learns about the differences between the sexes, and the birth of children and roles of men and women in society and family.
6. Realizing man is nothing without money, power, property, or rank, the creature thinks more about where he came from. The creature realizes that he does not possess any qualities (wealth, beauty, intelligence) which are valued by man and feels that he is "a blot upon the earth, from which all men fled, and whom all men disowned". He realizes that he truly has nothing—no friends, no money, no property, and that he is a monster and is doomed to be rejected from society. Finally, he realizes he has no one— no family or companionship to speak of—and feels painfully lonely and dejected.
7. The creature's desire to interact with others and have a family show that he has the capability to be human instead of cruel. He does not want to harm others, but to be included as a member of a family.

Chapter Fourteen

1. The De Laceys were a well-to-do, highly respected family in Paris. Felix served his country, and Agatha moved throughout high society.
2. Safie's father was a Turkish merchant, who suddenly became an enemy to the government of France. He was arrested and put into prison, tried, and condemned to death. It was said that he was an enemy because of his religion and nothing else. Upon hearing this, Felix became enraged and vowed to help the Turk escape. In return, the Turk offered wealth, but Felix saw Safie and thought that she would be a good reward.
3. The Turk says that he will give Safie's hand in marriage to Felix if he will help him escape.
4. Safie wants to marry a Christian, as she was taught Christianity by her mother, and live independently and make her own decisions. She does not want to live in a harem without any rights, "allowed only to occupy herself with infantile amusements."
5. Safie's father fell in love with and married a Christian Arab, but he will not allow Safie to marry a Christian.
6. De Lacey and Agatha are arrested and put in jail for Felix's aid in the escape. Felix learns of this and returns home to Paris. The entire family is put on trial, found guilty, and forced

into exile in Germany, stripped of everything they once had.

7. *Answers will vary. Students should provide details to support their answers.* Some students may feel that Felix and Safie's love made the De Lacey family's troubles worthwhile, while other students may question why the De Laceys chose to risk their lives and fortune for someone they barely knew.

8. *Answers will vary.* The letters should demonstrate Safie's independence and unwillingness to be placed in a harem.

Pages 67-69: Standards Focus: Political and Philosophical Approach

1. *Answers will vary. Sample answers include:* Napoleon banished, Congress of Vienna, Brazil and Argentina gain independence, Malthus' *An Inquiry into the Nature and Progress of Rent,* painters Goya and Turner, Prout's research on the relationship between specific gravity and atomic weight, English postwar economic crisis, first steam warship-U.S.S. Fulton, Prince Metternich opens Diet of Germany, Indiana becomes a U.S. state, Jane Austen's *Emma,* Shelley's *Alastor,* Byron's *The Siege of Corinth,* invention of kaleidoscope and stethoscope, Volney's *Ruins of Empires* conveys the radical thoughts of revolutionary and Napoleonic senator Volney

2. a. The Turk was convicted because of his wealth and religion; it is implied that he is not a Christian.
   b.   Shelley implies that the Turk was tried and condemned for racist, rather than legal, reasons. He was also tried and condemned the same day. It is assumed that he did not receive legal representation, time to research his case and call witnesses, nor the opportunity to appeal his sentence.
   c.   In Justine's conviction, she was also tried and put to death quickly without legal representation or the opportunity for an appeal.

3. a. Safie wants to live independent and openly in society.
   b.   She refers to women's activities as "infantile amusements" and implies that women should pursue more "grand ideas and a noble emulation of virtue".

4. Safie chooses to disobey her father by traveling on her own to meet Felix. This demonstrates women's ability to think and act independently.

Pages 70-71: Assessment Preparation: Word Origins—Etymology

Student sentences will vary. Possible answers for other words containing the word root are provided.

1. dissipates: a. scatters in various directions; dispel, disperse
2. cadence: d. rhythmic flow of sounds or words; cadences; cadency, accident, cadaver, cascade, cheat, decay, occident
3. scion; b. descendant or offshoot; shoot, sprout, split
4. vagabond: d. person who wanders from place to place; vagrant, wander, walk
5. tenets: d. doctrines; tendon, tenuous, tenacious
6. immured: c. confined; mural, wall
7. noisome: b. offensive; annoy, noise, nausea, odious
8. expostulate: a. reason earnestly; posit, expository, expose
9. pittance: c. small amount; piety, pity, portion

Page 73: Chapters Fifteen—Sixteen: Note-Taking and Summarizing

Each set of chapters has at least one page for this activity. See *Summary of the Novel* (pp. 127-129) for possible answers. *Student answers will always vary.*

Page 74: Chapters Fifteen—Seventeen: Comprehension Check
Chapter Fifteen

1. When reading *The Sorrows of Werter,* the creature ponders his place in the world and how he fits in—he was left feeling despondent and depressed. *Plutarch's Lives* teaches him about history and people outside of himself and his world; he learns to respect and admire the men before him.

2. Adam is created, cared for, and communicates with a loving creator. The creature was abandoned by Victor, his creator, and feels lonely and bitter.

3. Knowledge shows the creature how much of an outcast he is from society, and how difficult it will be to become an accepted member of society.

4. The creature thinks the DeLacey family will be kind and compassionate, overlooking his hideous deformities.

5. The older man listens to the creature and is kind to him. When Felix returns home to find the creature, he beats him until he leaves the cottage.

6. *Answers will vary.* It may have helped if the creature took the introduction more slowly,

forming a relationship with the older man before meeting the rest of the family. He could have also told them how he was the one helping gather wood and tend the farm.

Chapter Sixteen

1. "There was none among the myriads of men that existed who would pity or assist me; and should I feel kindness towards my enemies? No: from that moment I declared everlasting war against the species, and, more than all, against him who had formed me, and sent me forth to this insupportable misery." (135) *Answers will vary. Sample answer:* This is definitely a turning point for the creature. I feel sorry for him, that his one hope of acceptance—the DeLacey family—has rejected him just like Victor did. I think that this moment will make the creature even more angry and hateful. All hope is lost.

2. After thought, the creature admits that he should have introduced himself slowly to the family, winning the trust and companionship of the father first, then revealing himself to the rest of the family. He vowed to go back to the father to reintroduce himself to him and take it slowly.

3. After noticing the cottage is empty, he sees Felix discussing leaving with his landlord. Although they have 3 months of paid rent and a garden full of food, Felix says they cannot stay. As result, the creature is angry and burns the garden and cottage to the ground, then runs away.

4. The creature feels that Victor is the person most likely to offer him companionship and a way to improve the creature's feelings of injustice.

5. Before the incident with the DeLacey family, the creature thought of humans as good and caring. After the incident, he is bitter and wants revenge, especially on Victor.

6. The creature happened upon a girl playing, when she slipped and fell into the river. The creature came out of his hiding spot and saved her, just as a man saw him. The man thought the creature was hurting her, took the girl, and went after the creature, shooting and injuring him. While Shelley keeps offering us a glimmer of hope for the creature, mankind acts with hatred, again and again. In this case, the creature was being benevolent, and he was shot at as a result. This further fuels the creature's hatred and want for revenge against his creator.

7. At first, the creature hopes to find a friend in the boy, deciding that he is too young make judgments about him. The boy struggles to

get away from the creature, revealing who he is, and the creature chooses to kill him as a way to hurt and gain revenge against Victor.

8. The creature places the locket in Justine's pocket as revenge for his lack of female love and companionship.

9. The creature demands that Victor make him a female companion of the same species and with the same deformities.

Chapter Seventeen

1. Victor first responds that he will not make a mate for the creature, no matter the threat or torture that ensues.

2. The creature tells Victor that as his creator it is Victor's responsibility to make him happy. The creature also says that he and his mate will move far away from humans and will not harm anyone.

3. The creature believes that his vices result from his loneliness, and that his virtues will shine through if he has a companion.

4. The creature will watch Victor and reappear when his mate is complete.

5. Both the creature and Walton express a strong, desperate desire for companionship.

6. *Answers will vary.* Reasons to create a mate: believing the creature's assertion that he and a mate will live apart from humans, prevent more harm to Victor's family; Reasons to not create a mate: no guarantee that the creature and the mate will not harm anyone, no guarantee that the mate will stay with the creature.

Pages 75-76: Standards Focus: Point of View

1. *Answers will vary. Possible answers include:* reads literature (127), reacts with emotion to what he reads (127), wonders about his beginnings and purpose in life (128), wants to commune with his creator like Adam does (129), hurt that Victor is repulsed by him (130), decides to reach out to DeLacey family (130), wants to be part of a family (131), concerned about his appearance (131), loves DeLacey family (133)

2. *Answers will vary.* Most readers want the creature to find kindness and companionship with the DeLacey family. Thus, readers will feel hopeful when reading about the DeLacey father's reaction to the creature and show disappointment in Felix's reaction. Readers will also feel sorry for the creature. By previously using the creature's point of view to show his humanity and desire for companionship, the creature elicits sympathy from the reader when he is thrown out by the DeLacey family.

3. **Victor's version of crime:** killed because of locket; creature searched for William with intent to kill him; creature knew who Justine was when framed her; **Similarities in stories:** killed because of relationship to Victor; killed out of spite; locket intentionally placed in Justine's pocket; Victor knows who the true murderer is; location of murder; strangles William; **Creature's version of crime:** creature hurt by William's comments about his appearance; places locket in Justine's pocket as revenge for his lack of female companionship

4. *Answers will vary by student.* Be sure that students explain why they do or do not believe aspects of the creature's story.

Pages 77-78: Assessment Preparation: Clauses

1. Subject: I; Verb: resolved; Adjective clause: which would decide my fate; Relative: which
2. Subjects: I, I; Verbs: did pretend, inclined; Adjective clause: whose extinction I wept; Relative: whose
3. Subject: I, I; Verbs: saw, quitted, escaped; Adverb clause: when overcome by pain and anguish; Subordinating Conjunction: when
4. Subject: I; Verb: did extinguish; Adjective clause: which you had so wantonly bestowed; Relative: which
5. Subject: I; Verb: directed; Adverb clause: when my hunger was appeased; Subordinating Conjunction: when
6. Subjects: I, I; Verbs: placed, waited; Adverb clauses: as night advanced; after having destroyed every vestige of cultivation in the garden; until the moon had sunk Subordinating Conjunctions: as, after, until
7. Subjects: I, I; Verbs: could hope, felt; Adverb clause: although towards you I felt no sentiment but that of hatred; although
8. Subject: It; Verbs: was; Adverb clauses: when I quitted the district, where I had so long resided; Subordinating Conjunctions: when, where
9. Subjects: child, I, he; Verbs: struggled, loaded, grasped, lay; Adjective clause: which carried despair to my heart; Relative: which
10. Subjects: I, I, I, I; Verbs: was overcome, left, had committed, entered; Adverb clauses: while I was overcome by these feelings, where I had committed the murder; Subordinating Conjunctions: while, where; Adjective clause: which had appeared to me to be empty; Relative: which
11. Subjects: I, he; Verbs: shall respect, contemns; Adverb clause: when he contemns me; Subordinating Conjunction: when

Page 79: Chapters Eighteen—Twenty: Note-Taking and Summarizing
Each set of chapters has at least one page for this activity. See *Summary of the* (pp. 127-129) for possible answers. *Student answers will always vary.*

Page 80: Chapters Eighteen—Twenty: Comprehension Check
Chapter Eighteen
1. Alphonse Frankenstein thinks that Victor does not want to marry Elizabeth, that he regards her as more of a sister, and that he is in love with someone else.
2. Victor feels that he must complete the task of building a female creature before he can marry Elizabeth.
3. Victor tells his father that he wants to travel to England before he marries. Victor does not tell his father that the journey will give him time and resources to build the creature.
4. Victor thinks the monster will follow him to England and not harm the Frankenstein family in Switzerland.
5. Unable to relax and think of anything but his task at hand, Victor was miserable up until the riverboat trip. Finally, Victor succumbs to the beauty of the trip and relaxes and enjoys the tranquility of the river cruise.
6. Victor appreciates Clerval's devoted friendship and imagination which always "soothes" his "heart."

Chapter Nineteen
1. Victor says, "a blight had come over my existence" and "I saw an insurmountable barrier placed between me and my fellow-men."
2. Clerval is occupied with working on making connections towards the progression of colonization and trade with India.
3. Victor views the process "like the torture of single drops of water continually falling on the head."
4. This is a reference to Victor seeing the lightning bolt hit the tree so long ago. He means that he is not the man he used to be—peaceful, content, and happy. He is now miserable, "wrecked," and hateful to himself.
5. Victor cannot stand anything associated with the creature, and Chamounix is where he listened to the creature's story.
6. Victor fears the monster will murder Henry as punishment for Victor's delay in the creation of the female monster.
7. That he stay with his friends in Scotland while Victor tours on his own. Victor wants to find a

remote place to build the woman creature alone.

8. The Orkney Islands are barren and remote. Just as the locale contains little life, Victor feels that he must complete his task alone. The task also makes Victor feel emotionally barren.

9. Victor does not really want to create a female monster. At times he cannot bear to enter the lab, but at other times he works for extended periods of time. He is disgusted by the work he is doing, but continues out of fear of the monster.

Chapter Twenty

1. Victor does not know how the female monster will feel and act. She may refuse to stay with the male creature; she may be more violent than the male creature; the creatures may have children together and begin an entire race of monsters.

2. When the male creature appears at Victor's window and Victor realizes his "malice and treachery," he destroys the female monster.

3. The monster calls Victor his slave and reminds Victor that he can make his life miserable. He also says, "You are my creator, but I am your master; obey!"

4. *Answers will vary, but may include:* the monster plans to haunt Victor and his wedding party; the monster plans to kill Victor on his wedding-night; the monster plans to kill Elizabeth on her wedding-night to Victor.

5. Victor keeps hearing the monster's threat in his head as he walks along the deserted beach. He regrets not going after him. He wonders what the creature will do on his wedding-night. Victor debates whether he should return home or stay on the Orkney Islands.

6. *Answers will vary.* Be sure students provide logical reasons to support their answers. *Sample answer:* If Victor had created a female monster, he could not guarantee how the two monsters would have acted toward each other and other humans. Creating another monster would also have held Victor hostage to constant demands by the monsters.

7. Victor takes the remains out to sea and throws them overboard with stones to weigh them down.

8. Victor lies down in the bottom of the boat and goes to sleep.

9. *Answers will vary.* Some students may predict that the monster's remains washed up on the beach, while others may believe the creature killed someone in the town.

Pages 81-82: Standards Focus: Characterization
Answers may vary. Sample answers are provided.

1. p. 153: *During my absence I should leave my friends unconscious of the existence of their enemy, and unprotected from his attacks, exasperated as he might be by my departure. . . my present sensations strongly intimated that the fiend would follow me, and exempt my family from the danger of his machinations;* indirect characterization; Victor is willing to sacrifice his own peace of mind for the safety of his family and friends.

2. p. 159: *During my youthful days, discontent never visited my mind; and if I was ever overcome by ennui, the sight of what is beautiful in nature, or the study of what is excellent and sublime in the productions of man, could always interest my heart, and communicate elasticity to my spirits. But I am a blasted tree; the bolt has entered my soul; and I felt then that I should survive to exhibit, what I shall soon cease to be- a miserable spectacle of wrecked humanity, pitiable to others, and intolerable to myself.;* indirect characterization; Creating the male monster changed Victor from a typical man into one who loathes himself and feels separated from the rest of humanity.

3. p. 163: *But now I went to it in cold blood, and my heart often sickened at the work of my hands. Thus situated, employed in the most detestable occupation, immersed in a solitude where nothing could for an instant call my attention from the actual scene in which I was engaged, my spirits became unequal; I grew restless and nervous. . . I looked towards its completion with a tremulous and eager hope, which I dared not trust myself to question, but which was intermixed with obscure forebodings of evil, that made my heart sicken in my bosom.;* direct characterization; Victor forces himself to work on the female monster, but is disgusted by the process.

4. p. 166: *"The hour of my irresolution is past, and the period of your power is arrived. Your threats cannot move me to do an act of wickedness; but they confirm me in a determination of not creating you a companion in vice. Shall I, in cool blood, set loose upon the earth a demon, whose delight is in death and wretchedness? Begone! I am firm, and your words will only exasperate my rage.";* direct characterization; Victor chooses to face the creature's wrath rather than create a female creature who may choose to harm others.

5. p. 168:" . . . when I awoke, I again felt as if I belonged to a race of human beings like myself, and I began to reflect upon what had passed with greater composure; yet still the words of the fiend rung in my ears like a death-knell, they appeared like a dream, yet distinct and oppressive as a reality."; indirect characterization; Victor feels better about himself since he refused to create another monster, but worries about the recourse the monster will take in regards to his family and friends.

Sample Character Sketch: *Victor does not want to create a female monster, but agrees to do so since he thinks it will protect his family and friends from the male monster's wrath. In this way, Victor shows his willingness to sacrifice himself for those he loves. Since creating the male monster, Victor has felt separated from the rest of humanity and feels he can reenter the human race when he refuses to create another monster. Victor's refusal makes him feel personally better about himself, but causes him great anguish regarding the safety of his loved ones.*

Pages 83-84: Assessment Preparation: Base Words/ Word Roots/ Affixes
Students' sentences will always vary.
1. a. franchise; b. en-, -ed; c. *enfranchir*—to free; d. verb; set free, liberated
2. a. sedulous; b. none; c. *sedulous*—diligently, without guile; d. adjective; diligent in application or attention
3. a. variegate; b. –ed; c. *variegates*—to vary the appearance of; d. adjective; marked with patches or spots of different colors
4. a. eminent; b. -ly; c. *eminere*—to stick out, project; d. adjective; prominently, high in station or rank
5. a. blight; b. none; c. origin unknown; d. noun; any cause of impairment, destruction, ruin, or frustration
6. a. precarious; b. none; c. *precarious*—obtained by asking or praying; d. adjective; exposed to or involving danger
7. a. profound; b. –ity; c. *profundus*—deep; d. noun; great depth
8. a. potent; b. im-, -ence; c. *impotentia*—want of self-control, weakness; d. noun; lack of self-restraint
9. a. exorable; b. –in; c. *exorare*—to prevail upon; d. adjective; not to be persuaded, moved, or affected by entreaties

Page 85: Chapters Twenty-One—Twenty-Three: Note-Taking and Summarizing
Each set of chapters has at least one page for this activity. See *Summary of the Novel* (pp. 127-129) for possible answers. *Student answers will always vary.*

Page 86: Chapters Twenty-One—Twenty-Three: Comprehension Check
Chapter Twenty-One
1. The black mark of fingers on the body's neck show that it was strangled.
2. Victor shows up in town around the time of the murder in a boat similar to one spotted near the crime scene.
3. Henry Clerval
4. Upon seeing Clerval's body, Victor becomes extremely agitated. While in jail, he becomes very sick and delirious and longs to die.
5. Mr. Kirwin sends a nurse to care for Victor; he writes to Victor's father; he defends Victor in court when he realizes the evidence proves Victor's innocence.
6. *Answers will vary.* Some may think that Victor thinks the creature will eventually murder him, others may formulate that Victor must by all means murder the creature.
7. It is proven that Victor was on the Orkney Islands at the time of Clerval's murder; three months
8. Although sometimes he wishes to be taken back to his innocent childhood years, Victor is depressed and suicidal because he holds himself ultimately responsible for Clerval's murder.

Chapter Twenty-Two
1. Victor created the monster's hands that murdered William and Henry and framed Justine for William's murder.
2. Victor feels responsible for the murders and would sacrifice his life to stop them. He would not, however, create another monster which could harm more humans in order to give in to the male creature's demands.
3. Elizabeth thinks Victor may have fallen in love with someone else and does not want to marry Elizabeth.
4. Victor thinks he and the monster will fight each other until one of them dies. He imagines his feelings of freedom when he is victorious. *Answers may vary.* He fails to consider that he may lose and the monster will kill him, or that the monster is out to kill Elizabeth.
5. *Answers will vary.* Students should justify how many or how few details they think Victor would tell Elizabeth regarding the monster.

Sample answer: When telling Elizabeth about the monster, Victor would most likely downplay his role in the monster's creation and focus more on the independent actions of the creature.

6. *Answers will vary.* The monster murders Elizabeth, rather than Victor.
7. Victor constantly carries pistols and a dagger.

Chapter Twenty-Three
1. A storm blows in just before Elizabeth is murdered.
2. The monster murders Victor's bride on her wedding-night. As victor discovers her, the monster, jeering grin on his face, points at her body then escapes through the window.
3. Victor worries that the monster will go to Geneva to harm other members of his family.
4. Alphonse dies soon after due to heartbreak and stress over Elizabeth's murder.
5. Victor decides to pursue the monster wherever he may go, and kill him when he finds him.
6. The magistrate thinks the monster is too strong and too quick to be caught by humans and that he may already be far away from the area.
7. Victor views the creature as an animal, not human in any way.
8. Ironically, it was Victor's pride of wisdom that got him into this situation in the first place so long ago.

Pages 87-88: Standards Focus: Historical Themes and Issues
Answers may vary. Sample answers are given.
Part One: Writes Victor a letter asking if he loves another (185), describes herself as tranquil if she marries Victor (186), Victor calls Elizabeth a treasure (187), Victor plans to tell Elizabeth about the monster after they are married (187), Victor says he knows Elizabeth "will comply" with his request (187), Victor does not consider how Elizabeth would feel or cope if he were killed (189), Alphonse has some of Elizabeth's inheritance restored (189), Elizabeth does not ask Victor about his secret (190), Elizabeth's mood alternates between joy and melancholy (191), Elizabeth dies without a fight (193), Victor plans to avenge Elizabeth's death (198)
Part Two: 1. According to the letters, Elizabeth stays at home without traveling or venturing into the world. She seems to be a passive woman who waits at home while the world goes on around her. She allows Victor to do what he wants while she just waits patiently for his return. Their relationship is most likely typical for the time period, as women are not often allowed to travel alone, nor are they able to go to school, let alone travel to "see the world."

2.a. Victor controls the relationship and expects Elizabeth to obey him and respect his plans, disregarding her thoughts on the matter.
   b. *Answers will vary*, but most students would probably want to know the secret before they were married. If the secret is too horrible, the person would then have the option of not getting married. Others may not care, citing that they always have the option of divorce.
3. *Answers may vary.* Victor does not consider how Elizabeth will fare emotionally or financially if he dies on their wedding-night, or that the monster may kill Elizabeth instead of him.
4. Since Victor was to be Elizabeth's protector, he feels more personally violated by her death. He has also loved her from childhood.
5. Essays will vary, but should discuss that all of the women in the novel (Justine, Caroline, Elizabeth) are portrayed as passive women who sit coolly by without arguing or interjecting themselves into the action, even if it directly concerns their own life, or is a case of life or death, as in Justine's case.

Pages 89-90: Assessment Preparation: Sentence Structure
1. I turned, I felt; dependent clause: who could utter so unfeeling a speech to a person just saved; compound-complex
2. physician came, prescribed, woman prepared, carelessness was, expression was marked; compound
3. father was, I was allowed and permitted; that I was again allowed . . . to my native country; complex
4. he thought, he endeavored; that I felt deeply the degradation . . a charge of murder; compound
5. I curbed, manners were; which sometimes . . . the whole world, than they had . . . to the sea of ice; compound-complex
6. he were vanquished, I should be; if he were vanquished; complex
7. he had vowed, he did consider, he was satiated, he had murdered; as if to show me . . . satiated with blood; compound-complex
8. I carried, was, gained; simple sentence with a compound verb
9. temper was fluctuating, joy shone, it gave; compound

Page 91: Chapters Twenty-Four—Continuation: Note-Taking and Summarizing
Each set of chapters has at least one page for this activity. See *Summary of the Novel* (pp. 127-129) for possible answers. *Student answers will always vary.*

Page 92: Chapters Twenty-Four—Continuation: Comprehension Check
Chapter Twenty-Four
1. He leaves Geneva and heads to the Mediterranean Sea where he boards a ship bound for the Black Sea. He then journeys north through Russia and to the Arctic Circle. He is searching for the creature, out for his revenge.
2. When he was hungry, he was able to procure food. When he was thirsty, it rained until his thirst was quenched, then the rain would stop.
3. Previously, the creature followed Victor as he traveled. Now Victor pursues the creature.
4. The creature enjoys the cat-and-mouse game with Victor. He also knows that the journey is difficult for Victor and uses this as a way to torment his creator.
5. The creature knows that he is in control of the journey and the "game" since Victor has to endure so much hardship to find the creature. While Victor pursues him, the creature is in charge and holds power over Victor.
6. The creature is obsessed with tormenting Victor and views humans as enemies. He does not hesitate to frighten or steal from people while on his journey, especially at the hamlet.
7. *Answers will vary. Sample answer:* Victor is not demonstrating rational thought or sanity. He continues pursuing a course that he knows will ultimately lead to his death via nature or the monster.
8. The ice breaks apart stranding Victor and his sled dogs on a floating piece of ice.
9. Victor feels that he is guided by the spirits of his dead friends and family. Victor also feels that after death, he will be able to guide Walton to the creature.

Continuation
1. The letters prove that Victor's story is true.
2. The ship is stuck between ice floes. The crew wants to turn around and head south. Walton fears a mutiny aboard his ship.
3. Walton has spent most of his time listening to Victor's story instead of tending to his ship and crew.

4. Victor chastises the men for wishing to abandon their "glorious expedition." He tells them that they will be hailed as "benefactors of the species...brave men who encountered death for honor and for the benefit of mankind" if they continue with their expedition.
5. *Answers will vary. Sample answer:* Victor has pursued the creature with as much vigor and strength as he can muster. He knows he is on his own "glorious expedition" to kill the creature or be killed himself. He does not want to be viewed as a coward, nor does he want to "lose" the game, so he fights on, recognizing the danger and excitement of the hunt.
6. Walton personally wants to continue north, but agrees to head south to avoid a mutiny.
7. *Answers will vary. Sample answer:* Since Victor abandoned the creature, he did not truly try to assure his happiness. His intentions were never to make the creature happy or assure his well-being—in fact, he only set out to avoid and/or destroy the creature from the very beginning.
8. *Answers will vary. Sample answer:* Victor would most likely have left the ship in pursuit of the creature, or convinced Walton to help him in his quest.
9. Walton finds the monster with Victor's dead body.
10. The monster mourns Victor and regrets hurting him. The monster also says that it hurt him to murder Victor's family and friends.
11. The monster claims that he felt compelled to harm others and could not avoid doing so. Since the monster chose to murder, this statement is not truly accurate.
12. The creature wants to die by himself.

Pages 93-94: Standards Focus: Themes
Answers will vary. Sample answers are provided.
1. **Knowledge for Good or Evil Purposes:** Victor tells Walton that his knowledge and ambition led to his ruin (208), Walton's goal of finding a passage to North Pole leads his crew into danger (12, 209), Victor becomes obsessed with "dark" knowledge while forming the creature (49), Victor's knowledge causes the deaths of William and Justine (86), Victor's creature murders Clerval (175), Victor's invention murders Elizabeth (193), creature becomes more forlorn after gaining knowledge (130), Victor's innate desire for knowledge (33), Victor acknowledges that his

desire for knowledge goes too far (35), Victor builds on previous scientific knowledge (45)

2. **The Desire for Companionship:** Walton expresses sadness at Victor's death (212), monster wants to die since his creator/ companion is dead (219), Victor's joy regarding his friendship with Clerval (34), creature wants to be a part of the DeLacey family (132-133), Felix is much happier when Safie arrives (115), Creature wants Victor to form a mate for him (145), Clerval calms Victor in Ingolstadt (58), Creature wants to fit in with human society (119), Creature refers to the DeLaceys as his family (127), Victor enjoys Clerval's companionship (152, 155)

3. **The Power of Nature:** Victor is intrigued when he sees lightning destroy a tree (38), Victor uses lightning to give life to the creature (55), Victor and Clerval's walks improve Victor's spirits (68), lightning illuminates the creature in the distance (75), Victor retreats to the middle of the lake for a respite (89), nature soothes Victor (92, 94), creature uses fire to destroy DeLacey's cottage (138), Victor enjoys journey along the Rhine (154)

Pages 95-96: Assessment Preparation: Analogies

1. disencumbered; installed and ensconced, as well as alleviated and disencumbered are synonyms
2. procured; clothes can be purchased, as Victor procured fish in the arctic
3. superfluous; indispensable and necessary are synonyms, just as extraneous and superfluous are
4. congeal; blood clots just as gelatin congeals.
5. repast; a fiesta is a type of party, just as a banquet is a type of repast
6. disposition; a person's character can be described as sketchy, just as one's disposition can be described as sunny
7. scoffing; a person may applaud a performance, just as someone may scoff at a criminal
8. contumely; compliment and flattery are synonyms, just as insult and contumely are
9. actuated: stopped and impeded are synonyms, as are motivated and actuated

Page 97: Quiz: Prologue and Letters

1. c. Percy Bysshe Shelley
2. b. Stoker's *Dracula*
3. d. self-control
4. a. Northern passage through the Arctic
5. c. a friend
6. a. Walton believes in the "marvelous."
7. c. a large man on a sledge

8. b. healthy
9. d. to relieve himself of his guilt
10. a. to take notes of the story

Page 98: Vocabulary Quiz: Prologue and Letters

1. c. concerned with the normal functioning of an organism
2. i. describing or outlining with precision
3. e. a means to an end; resource; method
4. b. strong inner feelings of a future misfortune or evil
5. g. to satisfy to the fullest
6. f. something which leads one on with a desire or hope
7. d. attributes of mind or body
8. j. concern over someone or something
9. a. look or expression of the face
10. h. a gloomy state of mind

Page 99: Quiz: Chapters 1-2

1. Victor's father, Alphonse Frankenstein, helped a friend, Beaufort, who had fallen on hard times. After Beaufort died, Alphonse cared for and married Beaufort's daughter, Caroline.
2. Victor enjoys an idyllic childhood and is doted on by his parents as they travel throughout Europe.
3. When visiting the poor, Caroline meets a peasant family who has taken in Elizabeth from a Milanese nobleman. The family can no longer afford to care for Elizabeth, so the Frankenstein family adopts her.
4. Clerval and Victor have been best friends since childhood. Clerval possesses a sunnier disposition than Victor and enjoys studying history and literature.
5. Victor becomes obsessed with reading the works of early alchemists (Cornelius Agrippa, Paracelsus, and Albertus Magnus).
6. Victor educates himself about alchemy and natural science.
7. Victor sees a lightning bolt destroy a tree and wonders about the power of lightning and electricity.

Page 99: Vocabulary Quiz: Chapters 1-2

1. reverential
2. indefatigable
3. tertiary
4. penury
5. ignoble
6. ineffectual
7. interment
8. chimerical
9. vehement
10. recompensing

11. **Page 100: Quiz: Chapters 3-5**
1. true
2. false; Henry Clerval's father does not think his son needs to attend college.
3. false; M. Waldman takes Victor under his wing and acts as his mentor.
4. true
5. false; Technology as a destructive, evil force appears repeatedly in the works of Romantic writers.
6. true
7. true
8. false; After the creature comes to life, Victor is disgusted and runs screaming from the room.
9. true
10. false; Henry asks Victor to write a letter to his father and Elizabeth.

Page 101: Vocabulary Quiz: Chapters 3-5
1. c. prognosticated
2. a. repose
3. d. repugnance
4. b. reprobated
5. a. recapitulation
6. d. deference
7. a. dogmatism
8. b. hinderance
9. d. incipient
10. a. languor

Page 102: Quiz: Chapters 6-8
1. At age 12, Justine lives with the Frankensteins after her own mother mistreats her. When her mother later becomes sick, Justine leaves the Frankensteins to care for her mother, but returns after her mother passes away.
2. William, the youngest Frankenstein child, has blue eyes, curly hair, and dark eyelashes. He has dimples and is a happy child. He seems to be between 7 and 10 years old.
3. Victor and Clerval begin studying the Asian languages of Persian, Arabic, and Sanskrit.
4. William is strangled.
5. Victor created the monster that murdered William. If Victor had not created the monster, William would most likely still be alive.
6. The locket containing the picture of Caroline Frankenstein is found in Justine's pocket.
7. Since he was not in town at the time of the murder, Victor believes that he will be viewed as a madman if he shares who he believes murdered William.
8. Elizabeth says that Justine acted as a mother to William and would not have hurt her. Elizabeth also says that Justine would not

have needed to steal the locket since she would have given it to Justine if she had asked for it.
9. Justine is bullied into confessing, but she also thinks that by becoming a martyr she will go to heaven.

Page 102: Vocabulary Quiz: Chapters 6-8
1. i. hateful; detestable
2. b. bearing or demeanor, as showing character or feelings
3. a. incapable of being remedied
4. h. calm or undisturbed
5. f. a funeral song which mourns the dead
6. d. state of violent excitement or emotions
7. g. state of being corrupt, wicked, or perverted
8. c. being open or sincere in speech or expression
9. j. discreditable; humiliating
10. e. approval; commendation

Page 103: Quiz: Chapters 9-10
1. b. becoming depressed and wanting to be alone.
2. d. rows his boat into the middle of the lake.
3. c. Both a and b
4. d. harm Victor's family members
5. b. Nature can act as a soothing healing force.
6. d. comply with the creature's demands or he will continue to murder people
7. a. Humans' abhorrence of him drove him to commit murder.
8. c. well-spoken and intelligent

Page 104: Vocabulary Quiz: Chapters 9- 10
1. precipitous
2. base
3. disdain
4. epoch
5. augmenting
6. diabolically
7. efface
8. pallid
9. abhorred
10. abyss

Page 105: Quiz: Chapters 11-12
1. true
2. false; The creature first learns about fire when he burns his hand in an abandoned fire.
3. false; The first humans the creature encounters treat him cruelly.
4. true
5. true
6. false; The DeLacey family lives in poverty and struggles to survive.

7. true
8. true
9. false; The creature observes the DeLacey family for several months.
10. false; The creature views the DeLacey family as superior to himself.

Page 106: Vocabulary Quiz: Chapters 11-12
1. b. opaque
2. a. emigration
3. c. inclemency
4. d. purloined
5. d. pensive
6. c. conjectured
7. a. venerable
8. b. enigmatic
9. d. ardently
10. c. arbiters

Page 107: Quiz: Chapters 13-14
1. Safie's arrival improves Felix's spirits.
2. The creature learns to speak as the family teaches Safie to speak and read French.
3. The creature only leaves his hovel during nighttime and stays away from villages and other areas inhabited by humans.
4. The creature realizes that he does not possess any qualities (wealth, beauty, intelligence) which are valued by man.
5. The De Laceys were a well-to-do, highly respected family in Paris. Felix served his country, and Agatha moved throughout high society.
6. The Turk says that he will give Safie's hand in marriage to Felix if he will help him escape.
7. Safie wants to live independently and make her own decisions, not live in a harem without any rights.
8. Safie's father fell in love with and married a Christian Arab, but he will not allow Safie to marry a Christian.

Page 107: Vocabulary Quiz: Chapters 13-14
1. b. green vegetation
2. h. scatters in various directions
3. j. rhythmic flow of sounds or words
4. g. a descendant or offshoot
5. d. person who wanders from place to place
6. a. doctrines held by members of a group, profession, or movement
7. f. secluded; confined
8. i. offensive; disgusting
9. c. to reason earnestly with someone
10. e. small amount or share

Page 108: Quiz: Chapters 15- 17
1. c. Coleridge's *The Rime of the Ancient Mariner*
2. d. the creature realizes how much he is an outcast from society.
3. c. by talking to the father while the rest of the family is out of the home
4. a. Felix beats the creature until he leaves the family's home.
5. b. The creature sets the DeLacey's cottage on fire.
6. c. The creature feels that Victor is the person most likely to offer him companionship.
7. a. He is shot.
8. c. The creature wants Victor to make him a female companion.
9. a. The creature would be less angry if he wasn't lonely.
10. d. The creature will watch Victor and reappear when Victor completes his task.

Page 109: Vocabulary Quiz: Chapters 15-17
1. wantonly
2. deprecate
3. malignity
4. instigate
5. succor
6. contemns
7. sagacity
8. vestige
9. epithets
10. consternation

Page 110: Quiz: Chapters 18- 20
1. false; Victor feels that he must complete the task of a building a female creature before he can marry Elizabeth.
2. true
3. false; Victor appreciates Clerval's company on the trip to England, but does not want Clerval to accompany him to the Orkney Islands.
4. true
5. true
6. false; Victor sets up a lab in a cabin on the Orkney Islands.
7. false; As the monster looks through the window, Victor destroys the female creature.
8. true
9. true
10. false; Victor lays down in the bottom of his boat and falls asleep.

Page 111: Vocabulary Quiz: Chapters 18-20
1. b. enjoined
2. a. impotence
3. d. profundity
4. a. enfranchised
5. c. precarious
6. a. eminently
7. c. blight
8. c. sedulous
9. b. inexorable
10. d. variegated

Page 112: Quiz: Chapters 21-23
1. Victor shows up in town around the time of the murder in a boat similar to one spotted near the crime scene.
2. Henry Clerval has been murdered.
3. Mr. Kirwin sends a nurse to care for Victor; he writes to Victor's father; he defends Victor in court when he realizes the evidence proves Victor's innocence.
4. It is proven that Victor was on the Orkney Islands at the time of the murder.
5. Elizabeth thinks that Victor has fallen in love with someone else.
6. Victor thinks he and the monster will fight each other until one of them dies.
7. Victor constantly carries pistols and a dagger.
8. The monster murders Victor's bride on their wedding-night.
9. Alphonse dies soon after, due to heartbreak and stress.
10. Victor decides to pursue and kill the monster wherever he may go.

Page 112: Vocabulary Quiz: Chapters 21-23
1. b. assumption; hypothesis
2. f. lacking in vigor or vitality
3. c. the face, usually with reference to shape, features, or expression
4. g. irritations; annoyances
5. e. lowered in dignity, character, or rank
6. i. intensely compelling
7. h. conquered or subdued by superior force
8. d. the act of clearly stating or declaring something
9. a. trickery; guile; cunning
10. j. state of dreamy meditation or fanciful musing

Page 113: Quiz: Chapter 24 and Continuation
1. c. They leave Geneva and head to the Mediterranean Sea where they board a ship bound for the Black Sea. They then journey north through Russia and to the Arctic Circle.
2. b. The creature leaves hints and clues for Victor.

3. d. The creature views humans as enemies. He does not hesitate to frighten or steal from people while on his journey.
4. a. The ice breaks apart stranding Victor and his sled dogs on a floating piece of ice.
5. c. Victor feels that he is guided by the spirits of his dead friends and family.
6. b. The ship is stuck between ice floes. The crew wants to turn around and head south.
7. d. Listening to Victor's story
8. b. Walton finds the monster with Victor's dead body.
9. a. The monster mourns Victor and regrets hurting him.
10. c. The creature leaves the ship.

Page 114: Vocabulary Quiz: Chapter 24 and Continuation
1. procured
2. abjuration
3. contumely
4. scoffing
5. congeal
6. repast
7. superfluous
8. disencumbered
9. actuated
10. dispositions

Pages 115-118: Final Exam
1. e. creates a human-like monster
2. i. family patriarch
3. a. younger brother of Victor Frankenstein
4. g. ship captain
5. c. wants a female companion
6. f. best friend of Victor Frankenstein
7. j. strangled on her wedding-night
8. b. beats creature until he leaves his home
9. h. defends Victor when he is accused of murder
10. d. executed for William's death
11. True
12. False
13. True
14. False
15. False
16. False
17. True
18. True
19. True
20. False
21. True
22. True
23. d. self-control
24. a. Northern passage through the Arctic
25. a. to take notes of the story
26. c. Both a and b